D1007647

NO LONGER PROPERTY OF
ANYTHINK LIBRARIES /
RANGEVIEW LIBRARY DISTRICT

BE ORGANIZED

《 RECLAIM **90 MINUTES** 》
OF YOUR DAY, EVERY DAY

Also by

MARIE RICKS

—— ⟫ ⟪ ——

BE ORGANIZED

RECLAIM 90 MINUTES OF YOUR DAY, EVERY DAY

‹‹ **MARIE RICKS** ››

PLAIN SIGHT
PUBLISHING

An imprint of Cedar Fort, Inc.
Springville, Utah

© 2018 Marie Calder Ricks
All rights reserved.

No part of this book may be reproduced in any form whatsoever, whether by graphic, visual, electronic, film, microfilm, tape recording, or any other means, without prior written permission of the publisher, except in the case of brief passages embodied in critical reviews and articles.

The opinions and views expressed herein belong solely to the author and do not necessarily represent the opinions or views of Cedar Fort, Inc. Permission for the use of sources is also solely the responsibility of the author. Permission for the use of graphics and photos is solely the responsibility of Cedar Fort, Inc.

ISBN 13: 978-1-4621-2210-3

Published by Plain Sight Publishing, an imprint of Cedar Fort, Inc.
2373 W. 700 S., Springville, UT 84663
Distributed by Cedar Fort, Inc., www.cedarfort.com

LIBRARY OF CONGRESS CATALOGING-IN-PUBLICATION DATA

Names: Ricks, Marie Calder, author.
Title: Be organized : reclaim 90 minutes of your day, every day / Marie Calder Ricks.
Description: Springville, Utah : Plain Sight Publishing, an imprint of Cedar Fort, Inc., [2018]
  | Includes bibliographical references and index.
Identifiers: LCCN 2018012299 (print) | LCCN 2018015975 (ebook) | ISBN
  9781462129195 (epub, pdf, mobi) | ISBN 9781462122103 (perfect bound : alk.
  paper)
Subjects: LCSH: Home economics. | Housekeeping.
Classification: LCC TX147 (ebook) | LCC TX147 .R479 2018 (print) | DDC
  640--dc23
LC record available at https://lccn.loc.gov/2018012299

Cover design by Shawnda T. Craig
Cover design © 2018 Cedar Fort, Inc.
Edited by Allie Bowen and James Gallagher (Castle Walls Editing LLC)
Typeset by Kaitlin Barwick

Printed in the United States of America

10 9 8 7 6 5 4 3 2 1

Printed on acid-free paper

This book is dedicated to all the weary, overwhelmed people who would give anything to walk instead of run, pace instead of panic, and approach life with methods instead of defaulting to their moods . . .

CONTENTS

It takes a lot of work to be organized, but it takes a lot more work to be disorganized.

» Use tools, systems, and routines
» Do the best you can

Clean out, clean up, and organize your possessions.

» Purge ruthlessly: Keep one, share one
» Use the ABC storage method
» *Action project:* Purge and organize the bathrooms
» Set up launch and landing pads

Achieve successful life management no matter the season of life.

» *Action project:* Conquer clutter
» Practice self-ordering as you go
» Ease your pain; help others do the same
» Take the hassle out of housework
» Learn housecleaning methods

—— >> << ——

AUTHOR'S DISCLAIMER

I have been teaching and writing about home organization since 1986. When reading this book, you may at times recognize concepts that seem familiar. It may be that I have spoken or written about them before under a different umbrella. It may be that you have learned about them elsewhere. Know that viable home organization principles are universal in application. I speak of many of these principles briefly but freely in this book to lay the foundation upon which to practice superior organization skills—all with the intent of helping you be more organized and save up to ninety minutes every day. If something feels comfortable, I encourage you to continue to incorporate it into your life. I will do the same.

— >> << —

INTRODUCTION

Some flowers look similar when they are budding, but when they bloom it becomes apparent certain flora have packed a lot more petals into the very same space. For example, compare the daisy and the chrysanthemum.

The two flowers are often the same size, grow in similar ground, and bloom with the same regularity. They start out as seemingly similar buds but become entirely different flowers. When they bloom, one produces a lot more petals from the same-sized bud.

So it is with personal organization. Some people take the same amount of potential time (the flower bud) and pack a lot more punch into their day (the flower). They get more done faster. They have more leisure time and can pursue their pleasures. They often experience more personal peace. They have a different, better life. The amount of time they have more nearly resembles a chrysanthemum than a daisy. This book is about this better way to live. It is about living like a chrysanthemum instead of a daisy.

You, too, can have more petals of time in your life. For example, if you become just 10 percent more organized, you can gain ninety minutes more time each day. Think about it. There are twenty-four hours in a day. Most people sleep approximately eight hours per night. That leaves about sixteen hours of living—the time when you are up, about, and doing. If you become just 10 percent more organized, you can gain 1.6 hours or approximately ninety minutes per day.

Over a year's time, this equals close to thirty-four 16-hour days. That's almost three extra days of time per month. It is worth the time and trouble to get organized. Just apply the easy-to-incorporate principles found in this book and regain up to ninety minutes every day—for the rest of your life.

Are you ready for this fuller, happier life? Let's go to work!

— » 1 « —

GET, BE, AND STAY ORGANIZED CONCEPTS

It takes a lot of work to be organized, but it takes a lot more work to be disorganized.

- Use tools, systems, and routines
- Do the best you can

Each chapter in this book will focus on different principles of organization. You will be invited to practice principles learned by purging and organizing an area of your home. Then you will be introduced to new concepts. For example, getting, being, and staying organized means a willingness to pay the price. It takes work and practice. It is sometimes frustrating and discouraging too.

First, you have to get organized. This usually means purging about half of the items in your home—in a systematic way, of course, and arranging your rooms to most effectively reflect your lifestyle preferences while still gaining organizational efficiency.

Then you will want to be organized. This means keeping these same rooms orderly and your life on track, despite and around the chaos that often pervades regular living.

Finally, you will want to stay organized. This means returning your environment to a state of orderliness after seasons of stress, trauma, or distraction, all the while managing your ongoing commitments. It is always a process. And sadly, there is no end to organizing—if you want to stay organized. You can go on vacation for a week or take a day off occasionally, but you must ensure your home is maintained, cleaned, and welcoming through constant, loving attention to organization principles.

Knowing this, you might get disheartened and want to stop reading this book partway through. But please stay with it. You may find that a lifetime of organization is worth a bit of discomfort while you purge and a few weeks of trepidation while you practice new skills. Gaining vital organization skills can help you regain up to ninety free minutes every day.

USE TOOLS, SYSTEMS, AND ROUTINES

When you organize any room and want it to stay that way, you consider three things: tools (the items that facilitate organization), systems (also known as techniques or methods), and routines (also known as timing). When you organize your personal or your family's life, you do the same thing.

Good examples of this are organizing bathrooms using helpful tools, training family members to use reasonable bathroom systems when cleaning, and working out the best routines or timing patterns for returning the bathroom to order.

The concept of tools, systems, and routines can be used over and over again as you approach the systematic purging and organizing of rooms, your personal life, and your family's lifestyle.

DO THE BEST YOU CAN

Organizing is hard work. It is sometimes confusing. You consistently need to do things that you may not know how to do—even while you want to be successful too.

You will need these skills through many seasons of your life, including getting organized while attending school, being organized at a new job, and staying organized when life presents you with difficult or frightening trials. While each situation brings its own unique challenges, some important concepts will help you maintain organization on life's path.

Learning curve. The time after entering into something new and difficult is fraught with stress and discomfort. These feelings can be lessened by acquiring new tools, trying out new systems, and establishing regular routines. This organization learning curve may seem to last a long time on your path to competence, but please be patient with yourself.

Midstream changes. As you become organized and your competence grows, you may be challenged by midstream changes. Such changes can throw a wrench into your attempt to stay organized. When they are discovered, it is important to adjust as soon as possible to the new scenarios and work to get organized anew.

Sense of ability. You may yearn for a lengthy period of time to enjoy your new found ability to stay organized, but while the top of today's mountain may have a glorious view, it seldom lasts long.

Imagine having a new child, getting good at taking care of your infant, and then finding yourself moving from one state to another to accommodate a change in your spouse's employment.

Suddenly, you are thrust into new and challenging situations. You're likely to experience a period of ineptness as you organize your new home and manage your growing child. During this initial phase, be patient with yourself while you work to get organized again. There will be mistakes, delays, and sometimes hesitation as you take on new responsibilities and reorganize yourself. This often leads to a season of feeling comfortable and better able to perform with peace and a sense of security—you have reached a place of organization.

But soon enough, more midstream changes will arise. Sometimes a positive change will offer new opportunities to make organizational adjustments. For example, your sister comes to live with you for a summer of part-time employment. At other times, you may experience a downward slide (for example, your child develops a chronic illness that causes upheaval in your daily routines)—but you still have an opportunity to readjust and get organized again.

Then you may find your pacing again and be able to function at a higher level, and you may even train others to function successfully under your leadership. Then, just when all seems to be working well and you are settled in your role, you may be thrown again into a season of doing what you don't know how to do. For example, your sister returns to school or your child's health needs you to settle down, but your spouse's promotion demands traveling twice a month.

If you commit to doing the best you can—especially regarding personal organization—it would be best to be mentally ready. Anticipate a season of ineptness as you ground yourself and try out new organization tools. Plan on midstream changes that upend your organization systems. Don't get too comfortable in your organization routines; more challenges are inevitably on the horizon.

Be patient with yourself as you organize and reorganize to meet changing needs. Be tolerant, too, while others function as best as they can with their changing challenges. Getting, being, and staying organized is like a dance where there are always new steps to learn. It is time to begin.

— » 2 « —

CHAOTIC TO CONTROLLED

Clean out,
clean up,
and organize
your possessions.

- Purge ruthlessly: Keep one, share one
- Use the ABC storage method
- *Action project:* Purge and organize the bathrooms
- Set up launch and landing pads

This chapter shows you how to improve your personal environment and bring it to a new level of organization.

There are three main steps to moving from a chaotic home life to more organized surroundings: purge, use the ABC storage method, and set up launch and landing pads. Practice using these concepts by purging and organizing the bathrooms as your action project.

PURGE RUTHLESSLY: KEEP ONE, SHARE ONE

Most people keep up to 50 percent more items than are needed for a convenient and successful lifestyle. Do you too? If so, it is time to consider a better way: purging half of all you own (in other words, keeping one and sharing one). When you purge effectively, you discard, share, or appropriately store every item in your home. (While you may live in an apartment, condo, or house, the term "home" will generally be used in this book to designate your living arrangements.) The purging goal is to get rid of about half of all you own—keep one, share one.

KEY CONCEPT: When you tackle an organization project, you prepare in three ways: tools, systems, and routines. Tools are what you need to get the job done. Systems are your methods or techniques for performing the job. Routines are when and how you focus on the project at hand—the timing of your work. Carefully planning out the tools, systems, and routines that will be used with any organization project saves time and trouble.

Purging: Tools. Prepare for purging by gathering the supplies you will need to do a thorough job:

- **Medium-sized boxes.** Label at least one box for every room of your home. Use these to hold items that will be kept but should be stored elsewhere. Between purging sessions, these boxes are usually kept in the hallway or around the perimeter of a less-used room. You will be making a mess as you purge, but that is a necessary part of the process.
- **Fifty sturdy white 40-gallon bags.** These are used for items you plan to share with a thrift store or neighbor who needs the items more than you do.
- **Fifty sturdy black 40-gallon bags.** These are used for items you will discard.
- **Wastebasket.** This is for discarding the smaller items.
- **Garbage container.** This is for discarding larger items.
- **Cobbler apron with two large pockets.** Fill one apron pocket with supplies like a pair of scissors (for cutting) and a permanent marker (for labeling). Keep the other pocket for stashing small items that need a home elsewhere (such as paper clips, rubber bands, hair clips, and other odds and ends).

- **Trailer or truck.** This is for hauling away oversized debris and larger items you plan to share or discard.

Successful purging means (1) going through every drawer, cupboard, and closet, (2) getting rid of half of your possessions, and (3) returning the items to be kept to their proper places. You might start this massive but extremely important project by preparing simple Purging Plan forms (as in the following example) and then approaching the project in this order:

- List all the rooms in your home in the headers at the top of the form.
- List every shelf, drawer, or other storage area as a separate item under the appropriate room.
- Check off each area after you have purged it of unnecessary items.

The Purging Plan forms give you a written plan for this project. You may be at this for weeks or months. If you keep your completed Purging Plan forms in a binder and dedicate time each day or each week to purging, you can still keep up with your other responsibilities—and know exactly where to start purging next time.

EEE PLAN—EVERYTHING OUT, ESSENTIALS IN, EXTRAS GONE		
ROOM	ROOM	ROOM
SHELVES, DRAWERS, CLOSETS	SHELVES, DRAWERS, CLOSETS	SHELVES, DRAWERS, CLOSETS
☐ _____	☐ _____	☐ _____
☐ _____	☐ _____	☐ _____
☐ _____	☐ _____	☐ _____
☐ _____	☐ _____	☐ _____
☐ _____	☐ _____	☐ _____

Purging Plan forms for the kitchen, laundry, and half bath might look like this example. As each area within a room is purged, it can be checked off on the form.

For instance, you might have a laundry room with four areas of storage, so the form for the laundry room might have four boxes to check off next to the four listings. The half bath might have one cupboard under the sink with two shelves, a vanity, and some drawers, so that room will have three listings and three boxes to check off. The kitchen might need six listings and check boxes. This written plan will make it much easier to tackle a huge purge project systematically.

EEE PLAN—EVERYTHING OUT, ESSENTIALS IN, EXTRAS GONE		
ROOM	**ROOM**	**ROOM**
Kitchen	Laundry	Half Bath
SHELVES, DRAWERS, CLOSETS	SHELVES, DRAWERS, CLOSETS	SHELVES, DRAWERS, CLOSETS
☐ stove drawers	☐ over washer cupboards	☐ under sink
☐ sink drawers	☐ over dryer cupboards	☐ vanity
☐ mixing center drawers	☐ broom closet	☐ drawers
☐ stove cupboard	☐ drawers	☐
☐ sink cupboards	☐	☐
☐ mixing center cupboards	☐	☐

So prepare a template and make several copies of your Purging Plan form. Note the rooms you are going to clean out, and then walk through your home and list the shelves, drawers, cupboards, and closets that need to be addressed in each room. Put the completed forms in a binder or on a clipboard for ease of retrieval and for crossing off the check boxes. Schedule a bit of time each day (or a longer period of time each week) and lift the load of too much stuff from your shoulders. It is time! (A "Purging Plan Form" is available in the appendix.)

Purging: System. Purging consists of answering three questions and then moving the item in question to the proper box, bag, or wastebasket. These three questions help clarify how items would best be classified.

1) Is this item useful and needed? If so, it needs to either be put away in this room or placed in the appropriate labeled box for storage elsewhere.

Remember, the goal is to keep about half of everything—yes, the better half, but still only half. For instance, when it is time to address your kitchen's junk drawer, you will choose only the very best half to keep. The rest you can share or discard. If half of everything you own is eliminated, then the other half will likely become more precious, valued, and used.

As another example, you might take out all the towels from your linen closet and put them in separate piles on your bed. You will then return only half (yes, the best half) to your closet and let the rest go. The gained space will make your home feel larger and your soul less shackled with the unnecessary.

2) Is this item useful but not needed? If so, it needs to be shared.

You might be keeping things that are useful but no longer needed. Even though items are sound, workable, and sometimes valuable, they may have lost their purpose in your life. For example, especially when you get to the kitchen, it is time to find a new home for some of the unneeded pans, glass dishes, and cooking utensils. Freeloaders are no longer allowed. Only friends are welcome.

Guidelines make purging more organized and systematic. For example, put items to be shared in white bags. As they fill, double tie them to reduce "cheating." Cheating is second-guessing your initial response to the purging questions. And, yes, you might make a mistake and need some of these items in the future. So as you purge, keep a reasonable amount of such items as everyday dishes, pregnancy clothes, children's clothes, seasonal items, and frequently used tools.

3) Is this item not useful and not needed? If so, it can be discarded or recycled.

Put larger items to be discarded in the black bags. As they fill, double tie them to lessen "cheating." Tiny items can be deposited in the wastebasket. If possible, discard the items after each purging session or as shortly thereafter as possible.

When you come upon another family member's possessions, you can share the Purging Plan concepts with them and encourage them to find appropriate homes for treasured items, share useful but unneeded items, and toss those items that are both unneeded and not useful.

Purging: Routines. Remove needless distractions so you can remain focused, ruthless, and otherwise logical in your purging decisions. If you can find someone to watch your younger children, you could return the favor later. Also, try not to be distracted by the phone, doorbell, or media during your cleaning-out sessions.

Bring the labeled boxes to the scene of your current purging. If it's a really big project, you might have big white bags with a bag labeled for your sister, a bag for your neighbor, a bag for the thrift store, and a bag for the newlyweds down the street.

On the appointed day, begin to pull items out of the cupboard, the closet, or the room you are focusing on. Put anything that belongs elsewhere (in another room or in the storage area) in the labeled boxes.

Make good use of the wastebasket, the white (share) bags, and the black (discard) bags.

Please know that if you have stored something for a considerable time and haven't used it, it's time to give it away. It can be useful elsewhere but need not encumber your life any longer. Share it with a friend, neighbor, family member, or thrift store. Generously rid yourself of having too much of what you don't need.

Open your curtains to brighten the area where you are working, let in fresh air (if the weather is right), and get going. Tackle that closet, empty that cupboard, and even tackle that nonfunctioning room. You'll feel wonderful, gain new energy, and feel better about yourself because you have taken charge. It will take some time and trouble, but it will make for a great accomplishment. You can find peace and prosperity as you clean up and clean out!

USE THE ABC STORAGE METHOD

After successful purging, it is time to store your items. Taking advantage of space means storing frequently used items closest to the central part of your body, about elbow height. Store items you use less often above or below this height but within easy reach. Store items you use infrequently in less convenient places, such as places where you have to bend down, kneel, or retrieve a stool to reach a high-up place. You can refer to the different kinds of storing areas as "A," "B," "C," and "D" storage.

The "A" space for retrieval of items is between your shoulders and mid-thighs. You can easily visualize this area by putting your elbows to your sides and swinging your hands up and down in front of you. The most frequently used items are to be stored within this area. For example, in the kitchen, the top drawer under the counter and the bottom shelf of the upper cupboards are usually considered "A" spaces.

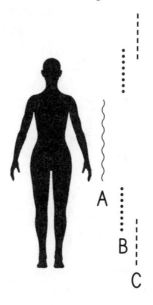

"B" spaces are farther from easy reach. Visualize this area by putting your hands as high as you can and then dropping your hands as low as you can without hunching over. Items used less frequently are stored in this space. In the kitchen, this usually includes the second drawer down under the counter and the second shelf up in the upper cupboards.

"C" spaces are still easy to get to but only with the aid of a small step stool or by kneeling or bending over. The bottom two drawers under the kitchen counter and the upper shelves in the kitchen are examples of these types of spaces.

"D" spaces are more difficult to get to and might include the convex corner shelves of your kitchen, either under or above the counter. "D" spaces also include any storage that requires a step stool or ladder (for example, the cupboard above your refrigerator). Store lighter, unbreakable items in upper "D" spaces and keep heavier or more fragile "D" items in lower "D" spaces.

And, of course, all storage must accommodate the safety of children. Storing chemicals or cleaning solutions of any sort within the reach of young children is irresponsible. Safety always outweighs organizational convenience.

When organizing the kitchen, bathroom, cupboards, closets, and garage, ask whether items belong in an "A," "B," "C," or "D" area. Then ask how you can best accommodate storing the items where they need to go.

Some areas of the home are easier to purge than others. Practice these concepts initially by purging "easier" rooms and thus gain traction to effectively reduce your possessions by half.

PURGE AND ORGANIZE THE BATHROOMS

You begin purging the bathroom by systematically emptying the closets and cupboards, wiping them down, and returning only those items that are both useful and needed. Then simplify the use of the bathroom by using "A" and "B" storage areas for items that help with bathroom projects. Keep surplus or less-used items in the "C" and "D" areas of the cupboards and closets.

As you organize the bathroom, turn shelving into easy-to-access drawer systems by using clear plastic containers for items such as makeup and hair-care products.

An "A" room in the home, the bathroom, is best organized to be a place for getting the job done quickly and easily returning tools to where they belong. Let's look at how to approach this need.

Bathroom: Tools. In the bathroom, each member of the family needs a place for personal tools. This includes a toothbrush, combs and brushes, shavers and blow-dryers, and bath towels. Personal tools need to be labeled with each person's name.

For example, if there is room, there might be a separate place for each person's towel—a "home" for their towel. In addition, each member of the family should have a colored towel or towels that have been clearly labeled with his or her name. This places direct responsibility on each person to hang up his or her own towel after it has been used. Using this same method, all bathroom tools need their own "home" and personal labels.

Bathroom: Systems. Each family member should know how to change the toilet paper, replace facial tissue, and put out a new bar of soap.

Family standards should include what the bathroom will look like after someone has used the toilet: Has the toilet been flushed? Has the lid been put down? Is there toilet paper still on the roll?

What will the bathroom look like after tooth brushing? Has the toothbrush been put back in its "home," the toothpaste put away, the sink cleaned of spittle, and the tap turned off?

What will the bathroom look like after a bath or shower? Is the bath towel hung up, the washcloth put in the dirty clothes bucket, and the shower curtain neatly spread out on the shower rod to dry?

Bathroom: Routines. The family can meet to discuss standards for bathroom routines. Then individual training and a practice session or two may be necessary to ensure that everyone understands the standards.

After that, someone in the family can be designated as the "sheriff" to help family members remember these duties. When family members are first learning, it may be necessary to use a "return and report" method for checking that the bathroom is up to standard after tooth brushing, using the toilet, or taking baths and showers. Learning to use tools, systems, and routines to keep a home organized makes for a smoothly run home and a happier family.

SET UP LAUNCH AND LANDING PADS

You would do well to also create launch and landing pads to organize the comings and goings of items. This will save time, frustration, and hassle. There is no home too small for the application of these principles. The three important concepts here concern where you will launch and land, the system by which you will launch and land, and the routines for your launch and landing.

Landing and launch pads: Tools. One of the challenges that may keep you from being more organized is simply the lack of designated places in your home for launch and landing. Yes, you have a kitchen counter where you put things if the counter isn't already "busy," but you may not have specific places free for launch and landing.

As an example, if you have a kitchen counter on which you regularly put groceries, this counter should always be relatively clear so there is an open place to put these groceries when you come in the door. This is a type of landing pad. One of your landing pads might be near your back door, another might be in your garage, and a third may be near the front door. Remember, a landing pad is a flat surface that is left empty for the items to be landed. Because you land something—and often many things—every time you return home, these landing pads will be well used.

Other useful landing pads are located in the master bedroom, master bathroom, and home office. In these rooms, it is usually best to make the landing pad a cupboard or drawer to keep visible messes to a minimum. Your master bedroom landing pad may be a master bedroom closet shelf that holds recently purchased gifts waiting to be wrapped. A master bathroom landing pad may be the cupboard that holds a year's supply of toilet paper, feminine needs, and vitamins. (See chapter 11 for more information on saving time by shopping by the year.) The office landing pad may be where you keep extra paper clips, printer paper, and tape.

If there is room, you may also want to have a landing place where you temporarily keep purchased items that need additional attention. This might be fabric for a Halloween costume, a craft kit for the children's summer use, or a newly purchased top that needs the buttons better secured. This type of landing place holds items until you have time to move them forward to usefulness.

In the same way, there needs to be a place for launching. This is where you put items you are going to take when you run errands, go to a meeting, or have other obligations.

If you don't know when you will be launching an item, choose a launching shelf within a cupboard. This will keep the item out of sight until you need it. But because mistakes sometimes happen, you might choose NOT to use a landing place near the back door to be your "today's errands" launch pad—or else you might walk right past your neatly stacked items and head off with everything you need to "launch" still sitting at home. Usually there's only one good "today" launch pad, and that is in your vehicle.

Landing and launch: Systems. After selecting launch and landing pads, you must think about methods for putting things away and for gathering things up. For instance, when you bring groceries home, do you not only put the groceries away but also take the time to put the bags or sacks in their designated spot? And do your receipts find their way to your special "receipt" receptacle? In other words, when you land, do you finish landing?

In the same way, do you have a method for gathering up and preparing to launch? For most people, it is important to have a sturdy, oversized bag or another container for each regularly repeated activity or project. For instance, there might be a preschool teaching bag (with manual, visual aids, crayons, and extra paper) or a bag for going to the dentist or doctor (with toys and children's books to read) or even another bag for yourself when you get your hair done (with a book or partially finished handicraft).

By having these "grab and go" bags in your launching pad, you will be ready to leave at a moment's notice—which happens all too often!

Landing and launch: Routines. Finally, you will want to think about launching and landing timing. Successful home managers allow time for launching and landing. Launching is the hardest of the two because you are usually so stressed and hurried that you don't want to take the time to think well or thoroughly. This means launching is best done early: the night before for a morning need, in the morning for an afternoon appointment, or earlier in the day for a need that night. It also usually means looking through the launch pad for a small errand you could add to your schedule. For example, if you return the borrowed sheet music along with other errands, then you won't have to make a special trip out later.

Try to allow a few extra minutes to wind up and launch before leaving—because you will usually think of some last-minute "to-dos." And allow enough time to come down or "land" completely after you arrive home from an activity, project, or emotionally draining situation—you need this time before you rev up for the next project or activity requiring your focus.

KEY CONCEPT: Taking little bits of "time" spaces for launching and landing, using launch and landing systems, and designating places for your launch and landing pads will make launch and landing a successful process as you strive for organization.

» 3 «

HAPHAZARD TO HABITUAL

Achieve successful life management no matter the season of life.

- *Action project:* Conquer clutter
- Practice self-ordering as you go
- Ease your pain; help others do the same
- Take the hassle out of housework
- Learn housecleaning methods

Moving from haphazard to habitual means eliminating poor living patterns in favor of strong routines for essential but uninteresting responsibilities. Then you can focus with confidence on life's more interesting projects.

Small changes can make big differences. Moving from haphazard to habitual entails increasing self-discipline in several ways. This chapter helps you develop small habits that will make a big difference in your life. Let's first address managing your clutter.

CONQUER CLUTTER

There are three basic kinds of clutter: incoming, rotating, and outgoing.

Incoming clutter includes anything that makes its way into your home but doesn't live there. Rollerblades and backpacks are not incoming clutter, but newspapers and junk mail are. Groceries are generally thought of as incoming clutter when they come from the store, but they become outgoing clutter when the leftovers are finally put into the wastebasket.

Incoming clutter management is a continuous process and requires great skill and focus. Reduce this type of clutter by restricting its entrance into the home. For example, stop at an outside garbage can after retrieving the mail and discard anything that you didn't ask for, isn't a bill, or doesn't look interesting. Then make sure incoming clutter has a designated home, such as a landing pad, until it can be processed.

Rotating clutter includes items that live in your home but are constantly moving around: clothes, shoes, laundry, and kitchen items. Clothes get dirty, are washed, put away, worn, and become dirty again. Dishes are used, washed, put away, and used again.

Rotating clutter is reduced as you learn and practice finishing. This means setting personal and family standards about when a process is done. For example, when is the laundry done in your home? When it is dried but still in the dryer? When it is on the couch waiting to be folded? When it is folded and has been put away? The closer your clean laundry items get to their appropriate places in closets, shelves and drawers, the less clutter there will be in your home.

KEY CONCEPT: Try to get your laundry back to where it belongs while it is still warm. This habit will save hours of time over the month and will help keep the whole home more clean and orderly. A neater home is harder for anyone to want to mess up.

Another good habit is to "clutter sweep" through your home several times a day (right before breakfast, lunch, and dinner). During this sweep, put away what has been put down without being put away. This is an especially good habit for when you are on the phone, and it also allows you to restore order in your home with minimum effort. If others have left the clutter out, you can work with individual family members to find answers, establish better habits, and reward progress.

Another challenge with rotating clutter is the accumulation of items on flat surfaces. Solve the cluttered countertop issue by validating several known facts. People (including yourself) are going to put items down. You want to help your family members put things down AND put them away (at the same time). This is what "finishing" is all about. It means making sensible decisions about tools, systems, and routines to keep this "rotating clutter" under control.

The following are some answers to rotating clutter:

Rotating Clutter: Tools.

- **A honey-keep drawer.** Convenient to the back door, this is a kitchen drawer where you and your spouse can keep daily "bring home/take to work" clutter, such as keys, change, and paperwork.
- **A purse or briefcase place.** This might be a hook on the back of the pantry door or a shelf near the kitchen desk.
- **A diaper bag place.** For those with young families, this might be a lower, larger cupboard for keeping these regularly used bags.

Rotating clutter: Systems. Next, tell your spouse about your new "systems" and ask for his or her cooperation. In the example of the honey-keep drawer, if the treasures are left out again, suggest for a second time that they would be just as safely kept in a drawer, thus freeing up counter space. If they continue to be deposited absentmindedly, they can be slipped safely into the honey-keep drawer for later retrieval with a minimum of fuss and conflict.

In addition, you could say, "I thought we might leave the diaper bag here, and I've created a place to put your backpack there."

Rotating clutter: Routines. Compliment daily successes of your spouse and anyone else in the family when they take these opportunities for clutter control. You are setting things up for a lifetime of order and anything they do to help you saves you time.

Last, watch for the trouble spots with your new tools, systems, or routines, and find additional fine-tuning answers. Does a trash can need to be closer to the back door? Would a larger set of key hooks keep the keys convenient and more organized? What about a plastic container for an upper cupboard for easier vitamin retrieval each morning?

As much as possible, cluttered counters should be left that way for no longer than a day. A week's worth of clutter is discouraging; a month's worth almost too much to handle. It is time to manage your rotating clutter.

Outgoing clutter is anything that will eventually end up in a wastebasket. This includes food scraps, empty soda cans, yesterday's newspaper, and last month's magazine.

Outgoing clutter is best managed by having a wastebasket in every room of the house. In this case, bigger is always better. Good places for another wastebasket are where people sit, where you stand, and where trash is "made." Teach your family members about getting the outgoing clutter on its way by making ample use of wastebaskets.

Empty most wastebaskets weekly, and empty the kitchen wastebasket daily. If your kitchen wastebasket gets overfull in less than one day, it is time to have two wastebaskets in that room. In fact, most kitchens could use two wastebaskets, both out in the open where they are easily used without having to open a door. One wastebasket could hold "non-wet" items such as packaging, plastic grocery bags, and bulk mail. This one won't need a liner. The other wastebasket should be lined and hold "wet" items. This second wastebasket should be nearer the sink, where "wet" items such as produce peelings are found.

An organized person sets up a regular routine for emptying waste-baskets—full or not. This job is therefore not left to be done haphazardly but is done by methodical habit. Have the best worker in the house empty the wastebaskets regularly. Remember, an empty wastebasket begs to be filled, which helps family members keep outgoing clutter going out.

Knowing that wastebaskets will be attended to in a timely manner also brings a great feeling of control into your life. It's one less stress and one more place of order in your life.

KEY CONCEPT: You probably won't have more time to read two magazines this month than you had to read one the previous month, so when the new magazine arrives, discard the last issue as you process your mail. Exceptions might apply if the magazines have reference material or patterns for hobbies.

PRACTICE SELF-ORDERING AS YOU GO

It is time to discover if you are living in a "halfway" house. Yes, your home may be full of items that are halfway to their rightful "homes." They have been put down but not put away. A beloved book is lost because it never made it back to its "home." A pair of shoes is useless because one shoe is missing—and even though your son remembers having his shoes on when he came in the back door, he can't remember where he took them off. The milk has soured because it was left on the kitchen table instead of inside the refrigerator. And on and on goes the list.

You may habitually put items down instead of putting them away. And you may find that others are following your poor example. If this is the case, decide to move from being haphazard in your approach to life by practicing finishing habits, and then look to teach other offenders.

The skills involved are simple to explain and a bit harder to implement: Learn to bring a room back to its original state of order. Flush the toilet and put down the lid when you are done, put the soda can in the recycle bin when you have finished your drink, and wash all the dishes after a meal. Much of the haphazardness in your life is simply a result of not bringing your environment back to a state of orderliness.

Designate homes. Designate "homes" for every item in your house, including much-used items such as keys, reading glasses, money, and credit/debit cards. When you get home from school or work, practice putting your personal items back in their designated homes.

The same skill applies when dressing and undressing. When you take off your top, decide whether to hang it up for another use or toss it in the laundry. Don't haphazardly drop it to the floor with the thought that you'll make a decision later. Put all clothing and shoes in their designated "homes" when they aren't on your body or need to be washed.

Educate others. Then educate all family members. "The extra packages of toilet paper are inside the door under the bathroom sink." "Milk goes on the right-hand side of the top shelf." "Empty soda cans should be put in the family room wastebasket." "Before you come into the house, put outside boots and shoes on the garage shelves next to the back door."

Even more wastebaskets. Having small wastebaskets in strategic places makes it easier to "put away" trash instead of cluttering up a room. Put a small wastebasket in the family room where you sit and hand mend, put another in the backyard near the barbeque equipment, and place one in the unfinished basement storage room to keep these areas neater. These "specialty" wastebaskets won't need frequent emptying, but they will keep each living area neater.

Convenience. If someone consistently puts something down instead of putting it away, that usually becomes the "home" where the item is looked for when it is needed next. Therefore, whenever possible, keep things in the *first* convenient place. For instance, vehicle keys will be "found" easier next to an exit than anywhere else in the home, because the farther you or other drivers get into the home, the more places the keys can be "put down" instead of being put away.

As you go about life, look for additional ways to self-order. Try to change one "put it away" habit for seven straight days. Watch order increase in your routines and extra time become available for your use!

EASE YOUR PAIN; HELP OTHERS DO THE SAME

Even as you improve the organizational qualities of your home environment, watch for simple but significant ways to ease your pain as a home manager. This can result in immediate time savings. For example, work with family members to leave the bathroom better looking than when they entered it, turn all dirty clothes right-side out and unroll socks, and get dirty dishes into the dishwasher after meals. These three skills, along with those specific to your home-management needs, are worth personal pursuit and a teaching moment or two.

Cleanup the bathroom. Beginning with yourself and then teaching others in your home, suggest that every person clean up after themselves. Practice these skills when using the bathroom (especially before leaving for work and school in the morning). This means putting away toothbrushes, toothpaste, shavers, brushes, combs, hair clips, and hair elastics. This small hassle will benefit everyone who enters the bathroom.

Even small children can learn to put away what they get out, especially in the most commonly used room in the house. Teenagers should not be allowed to leave their messes in the bathroom either. Neither should adults, for it is common courtesy to completely clean up after yourself in the bathroom. According to your personal situation, establish the new habit by rewarding yourself generously for cleaning up after yourself. Offer rewards to those who clean up after themselves for one day, then for two straight days, and then for a week.

Alternatively, gather leftovers from each day's mess with a promise to give the items back in exchange for a "small" job performed by the offender. The job can be more symbolic than difficult; it won't take long for the offender to understand the need to help. Use these and other fun ways to encourage change!

Work with all members of the family to keep the bathroom organized: carefully monitor its use by younger children, reward those who leave the bathroom looking better than when they entered, and compliment spouses who cooperatively exemplify these habits.

Turn dirty clothes. Start with yourself and then teach everyone else that those living in the home must turn their clothes right-side out before depositing them in the laundry basket. This includes shirts, pants, underwear, and socks. Somehow turning is easier if it is your own clothing. In addition, have everyone check their pockets for trash, tissues, and treasures. A moment of "cleaning up after yourself" by each person in the family will save many minutes at the washer.

Can everyone help? Yes—even stubborn teenagers and reluctant spouses. But what if they don't immediately get the vision of "ease your pain"? Once you have established the rules and given ample time for training (one day's laundry should be sufficient), wash only clothes that are turned right-side out. It will be painful for a day or two, but soon everyone will get the point. The launderer has enough to do without turning dirty clothes right-side out.

Put dirty dishes where they belong. After the main meal, take your dishes to the sink, rinse them off, and put them in the dishwasher. Then encourage all household members to empty their drinking glasses and scrape their plates into the wastebasket or disposal. Encourage them to put their dishes in the dishwasher or a sink full of hot, soapy water. If everyone does a little bit to clean up, the home manager's job will be minimized and dishwashing will be much nicer to contemplate. Set an example and then help your family members see how their small contribution makes for a big change. (A day or two of assistance from those who usually leave their dishes "undone" will help mightily!)

Personal improvement in the little things will "ease the pain" for yourself and your family. Implement these and any other small changes you feel will help. Start with one change at a time over the next week or two and you will be astounded how much time, frustration, and emotional drain will be eliminated! Set the example, train, follow-up on those who don't respond to the challenge, reward those who cooperate, and soon your home will be running smoother than ever.

Then you might even have a contest to see what other "ease the pain" projects your family can adopt to smooth out home-management needs for all.

TAKE THE HASSLE OUT OF HOUSEWORK

Systemizing housecleaning is one of the best improvements a home manager can make to save time.

Housecleaning: Tools. High-quality tools are essential for the successful running of a home. Purchase and use the best you can afford. For example, a 24"-wide mop will clean floors much quicker than traditional 12" mops, and if you decide on microfiber products, you will get an additional punch for your cleaning efforts. Make the effort to acquire high-quality cleaning tools. This is an additional way to save time in the long run.

Then create strong habits to reduce haphazard home maintenance. First, break bigger responsibilities into smaller, more regular jobs. Then decide on the systems (or methods) you will use to get the job done. Finally, settle on the routines (or timing) for approaching each job for your housing situation.

Housecleaning: Systems. Systematic housecleaning routines are essential for couples, busy families, and retired persons. Everyone who lives in the home should have daily and weekly household jobs. Young children can be involved with chores that need doing several times a day. In addition to helping out with daily and weekly chores, older teenagers and adults can also attend to monthly, semiannual, and annual chores with the assistance of younger household members.

Even though every home is different, adults can decide what jobs need doing, set standards for cleaning depending on current circumstances and cleanliness needs, and decide on timing. Ideas can be set down on paper to include jobs that need attention at various times: (1) multiple times every day, (2) once a day (neatening up), (3) every week (light cleaning), and (4) monthly, semiannually, and annually (usually deep cleaning).

KEY CONCEPT: Remember, individual responsibility promotes family functioning. Describe the jobs in minute detail to ensure everyone is fully informed and knows where their jobs begin and end.

The following ideas will help you set up a housecleaning plan in a home where preschool children can contribute to multiple-times-a-day household jobs. For example, preschoolers can

- Pick up toys before meals
- Prepare meals
- Clean up from meals
- Brush teeth after meals
- Neaten up the house before dinnertime

Daily jobs. Jobs needing older children's, adolescents', or adults' attention once a day might include these:

- **Morning**
  » Prepare and clean up from breakfast
  » Sweep the kitchen floor
  » Empty the kitchen wastebasket
  » Straighten the entry
  » Straighten the front room
  » Straighten the bathroom

- **Afternoon**
  » Prepare and clean up from lunch
  » Help children with homework
  » Prepare dinner

- **Evening**
  » Clean up from dinner
  » Help children take baths
  » Get children into bed

Weekly jobs—during the week. Some jobs only need attention once a week. If a spouse is home nearly full-time, these can be divided to focus on a few jobs each day.

- **Monday**
  - » Run regular batch of wash
  - » Vacuum the carpets

- **Tuesday**
  - » Wash the bathroom towels
  - » Clean the bathrooms

- **Wednesday**
  - » Run regular batch of wash
  - » Clean the kitchen

- **Thursday**
  - » Wash the sheets
  - » Run errands

- **Friday**
  - » Run regular batch of wash
  - » Dust the house
  - » Vacuum the carpets

- **Saturday**
  - » Mow the lawn (spring and summer)
  - » Clear the sidewalks and driveways (fall and winter)
  - » Empty wastebaskets

Weekly jobs—on Saturday. Other times, the family will cooperate to clean and organize the home on Saturday:

- **Dad**
  - » Run regular batches of wash (times three)
  - » Wash the bathroom towels
  - » Wash the sheets for each bed once a month
    - o Master bedroom—Week 1
    - o Teenage bedrooms—Week 2
    - o Boys' bedrooms—Week 3
    - o Girls' bedrooms—Week 4

- » Vacuum the carpets (except bedroom carpets)
- » Gas up vehicles

- **Mom**
  - » Clean the bathrooms
    - ○ Towels to laundry room
  - » Clean the kitchen
    - ○ Towels and dishcloths to laundry room
  - » Purchase groceries

- **Teenage daughter**
  - » Dust the home (except individual bedrooms)
  - » Mop entry tile

- **Teenage son**
  - » Mow the lawn (spring and summer)
  - » Clear the sidewalks and driveways (fall and winter)

- **Younger children**
  - » Empty wastebaskets

- **Everyone**
  - » Straighten own bedrooms
  - » Dust own bedrooms
  - » Vacuum own bedrooms
  - » Bring sheets to laundry room on that person's sheet-washing week

Deep-cleaning jobs—monthly, semiannually, and annually. Other jobs need less frequent attention and can be done every month, every six months, or once a year. These jobs might include the following:

- **Dad**
  - » Change furnace filters (every six months)

- **Mom**
  - » Clean ceiling fans and light fixtures (every six months)

- **Teenagers**
  - » Wash the vehicles (once a month)

- **Younger children**
  - » Sweep the porches (once a month)

- **Whole family**
  - » Wash the windows (every six months)

In a home with two working adults, the schedule might differ and jobs might be attended to less frequently. But all necessary jobs are assigned and accounted for between the parties.

Preschoolers should be involved with jobs multiple times a day. During vacation time, elementary school children can do multiple-times-a-day jobs (which should become a regular habit by the time they are in school) plus daily and weekly jobs. During school, that usually means a short morning and a short evening job during the school week, with bigger responsibilities on the weekend. Adolescents can have daily, weekly, and occasional household jobs, with increased job difficulty and length depending on their capacity.

The goal is to reduce the haphazard running of the home and move toward the habitual. Adults must understand that jobs need to be assigned, training needs to happen, and younger members need to return and report on the successful completion of their jobs before they are allowed to access media, engage with friends, or play outside.

Housecleaning: Routines. Housecleaning should be tackled in a precise order every day.

Daily jobs. Once decisions have been made about job responsibilities, it is helpful for the home manager to prepare a written chore list for the family's review. This can be done on a large chart on the kitchen wall. High-tech families can also create phone notifications as reminders.

Alternatively, if you are a stay-at-home adult, you might list jobs essential to your housecleaning and house-maintenance routine on separate 3" x 5" cards. For example, if you are a newbie stay-at-home manager, limit the initial number of daily jobs to twelve. This means that you will have twelve separate 3" x 5" cards prepared, each listing a separate job as part of your morning routine. As you practice and gain confidence, you will be able to do more jobs with greater ease. Pretty soon you will be just like that "super" home manager down the street—the one who always seems to have an immaculate house.

The goal for the first week of practice is to complete all "twelve" daily jobs each morning. This is how. Wake up in the morning and get the kids off to school, your spouse off to work, and the preschoolers settled. Then spread the housecleaning job cards out on your kitchen counter. Choose one job to tackle, do the job, and then turn the card over. This is a wonderful "game" for two reasons:

First, you may get distracted by the needs of your spouse and children. When you want to return to your chores, it takes a lot of effort to overcome the current mood, possible weariness, and frequent mental distraction. Having your chores listed on cards keeps you on track.

Second, when you have decided what to do each morning and listed those jobs on cards, the decision-making has already been done. Just finish those twelve cards and you will be done with all the "daily" housekeeping you wanted to do that morning. You don't have to decide what needs to be done next; you can just get going.

Weekly jobs. Once you have successfully completed your daily jobs for one week, it is time to tackle the weekly jobs. Again, you might list these jobs on the kitchen wall chart or create phone notifications. Or you can purchase a 3" x 5" recipe card box. Label blank card dividers with the following: Daily (which is where you will store the "daily" cards you have already prepared), Monday, Tuesday, Wednesday, Thursday, Friday, Saturday, and Sunday.

You will need an additional twelve 3" x 5" card dividers when you set up your deep-cleaning job system. These cards will be labeled January through December. Then take about twenty-five lined 3" x 5" cards and go to work listing jobs that need your attention on the various days of the week.

For example, label one card "Laundry" in the top left-hand corner. Then write how often you plan to do your regular laundry in the upper right-hand corner (for example, "Monday, Wednesday, and Friday."). Store this card behind the "Monday" divider for now.

Label a second card "Vacuum" and write how often you plan to vacuum in the upper right-hand corner (for example, "Monday, Friday"). Store this card behind the "Monday" divider.

Label a third card "Dust" in the upper left-hand corner, and write in the upper right-hand corner the day on which you plan to dust (for instance, "Friday"). Store this card behind the "Friday" divider. Continue with all the jobs you want to do each week by yourself or with your family's help. Once you have set up your weekly housekeeping system, you are ready to go again.

Each morning, complete your daily housecleaning cards first, placing them out on the kitchen counter and flipping each card over as the job is done. Then put these cards away and get out your weekly housecleaning cards for that day. Spread out your cards on the counter and go to work again. When these weekly housecleaning chores are done, put the cards behind the divider where these jobs will need to be done again. The daily cards are always completed first, with the weekly cards second. Finally, pull one of this-month's deep-cleaning cards and tackle that job (if there is still time before other pressures descend).

Deep-cleaning jobs. Again, list deep-cleaning chores on your kitchen chart or as phone notifications. If you have prepared cards for your daily and weekly jobs, you can also prepare cards for deep-cleaning jobs, which will be done less frequently (monthly, quarterly, semiannually, and annually).

You list the job in the upper left-hand corner of the index card and the timing in the upper right-hand corner of the index card. For example, a card for vacuuming the baseboards might be prepared for July and then filed behind the July divider. As time and energy allow (meaning your daily and weekly jobs are done), pull out a deep-cleaning job card behind this month's card divider and go to work.

With practice, you will consistently have a neat and orderly home that is regularly being deep-cleaned as well.

Working person's housecleaning plan. During some seasons of life, housecleaning needs to be done between everything else that is happening. Set up a work person's housecleaning plan when there is a part- or full-time worker outside of the home or when there is a variable schedule because of familial or other external demands.

As an example, let's relook at how stay-at-home persons might assign their jobs by the day:

> Monday = dust the house
> Tuesday = clean the bathrooms
> Wednesday = clean the kitchen
> Thursday = wash the linens
> Friday = vacuum the house

Working persons' schedules beat to a different drum, and thus housework should be approached in a different way to meet this need. Approach home-management needs using a numerical system. Yes, there will still be chores that need to be "done" on a regular basis, but the rest of the chores can be approached in numerical order depending on the other demands on the working person's time.

To alter the example above to meet a working person's needs, you would assign some jobs as "DOs," meaning they are done every day. This would include preparing meals and cleaning up afterward. Other jobs, however, can be assigned by number:

> 1 = dust the house
> 2 = clean the bathrooms
> 3 = clean the kitchen
> 4 = wash the linens
> 5 = vacuum the house

After completing the necessary "DO" jobs, working persons might get job #1 done one evening and then have to wait two evenings before an opportunity arises to finish jobs #2 and #3. Then three more days may go by before they can finish job #4, and finally Saturday arrives before they finish job #5. They can begin their rotation again with the new week and start with job #1. (And, yes, they might involve as many of their family members as possible to lighten the load and make the home run smoothly.)

If you choose not to use the kitchen wall chart or enable notifications on your phone, setting up a Working Person's Housecleaning Plan involves the purchase of some supplies and an hour's preparation.

Working Person's Housecleaning Plan: Supplies

- 1 index card box (sturdy with closeable lid)
- 200 lined index cards
- 20 index card dividers (blank) labeled:
  - » Daily DO
  - » Daily Chores
  - » Weekly DO
  - » Weekly Chores
  - » Monthly DO

» Monthly Chores
» Wash DO
» Wash Chores

» January
» February
» March
» April
» May
» June
» July

» August
» September
» October
» November
» December
» 20_ _

Purchase the lined index cards, the index card box, and the dividers. Label the dividers as above and use the following examples to prepare your Daily DO cards. These are chores that should be done every day. Prepare your Daily Chores cards. These are chores that are rotated through as you have time and opportunity, but might not get done every day.

Prepare your Weekly DO cards. Again, these are chores that should be done every week. Prepare your Weekly Chores cards. These are chores that are rotated through as you have time and opportunity, but might not get done every week. Monthly DO, Monthly Chores, Wash DO, and Wash Chores cards are prepared for use in the same manner. Some chores are essentials; other chores are tackled sequentially.

- **Daily DO**
  » Make beds = Daily DO
  » Start daily wash = Daily DO
  » Empty dishwasher = Daily DO
  » Fix breakfast = Daily DO
  » Finish daily wash = Daily DO
  » etc. . . .

- **Daily Chores**
  » Tidy living room = Daily 1
  » Tidy family room = Daily 2
  » Tidy kitchen = Daily 3
  » Tidy bathrooms = Daily 4

- » Tidy bedrooms = Daily 5
- » Tidy master bedroom = Daily 6
- » Empty trash = Daily 7
- » etc. . . . .

- **Weekly DO**
  - » Plan weekly menu = Weekly DO
  - » Prepare grocery list = Weekly DO
  - » Grocery shop = Weekly DO
  - » Run errands = Weekly DO
  - » Do yard maintenance = Weekly DO
  - » etc. . . .

- **Weekly Chores**
  - » Pay bills = Weekly 1
  - » Tackle paperwork = Weekly 2
  - » Balance budget = Weekly 3
  - » Vacuum/sweep living room = Weekly 4
  - » Vacuum/sweep kitchen = Weekly 5
  - » Vacuum/sweep master bedroom = Weekly 6
  - » Clean children's bedrooms = Weekly 7
  - » Clean bathroom mirror = Weekly 8
  - » Clean bathroom counter and sink = Weekly 9
  - » Clean bathroom tub/shower = Weekly 10
  - » Clean bathroom floor and toilet = Weekly 11
  - » etc. . . .

You will notice that the more complex chores are broken down into smaller jobs. This is to facilitate the smaller amounts of time working persons have for cleaning. So the bathroom might be started by cleaning the mirror while waiting for your ride in the morning, and then the counter, sink, tub, floor, and toilet could be cleaned in the evening when you return home from work.

- **Wash DO**
  - » Wash white clothes = Wash DO
  - » Wash mixed clothes = Wash DO
  - » Wash dark clothes = Wash DO
  - » etc. . . .

(Depending on circumstances, an empty-nester couple might do two loads a week, while a small family might do one load a day and a larger family up to three loads a day.)

- **Wash Chores**
  - » Wash master bedroom sheets = Wash 1
  - » Wash children's bedroom sheets = Wash 2
  - » Wash kitchen and bathroom towels = Wash 3
  - » Wash pajamas = Wash 4
  - » etc. . . .

- **Monthly DO**
  - » Prepare budget for next month = Monthly DO
  - » Prepare calendar for next month = Monthly DO
  - » etc. . . .

- **Monthly Chores**
  - » Clean vehicle inside and out = Monthly 1
  - » File paperwork = Monthly 2
  - » Write monthly emails/letters = Monthly 3
  - » etc. . . .

January–December Chores. Other chores are specific to the months in which they would normally be done. For instance, as a working person, you would make up cards to remind you to do seasonal chores during the appropriate months. For example, store lawn furniture in September, add winterizing fluid to the lawn mower in October, and purchase or find Christmas gifts in November.

Now that your Working Person's Housecleaning Plan has been set up, it is useful to establish regular habits to focus on these skills. So let's go to work and see how it will happen.

Daily DO cards. Every morning, pull out the Daily DO cards, lay them out on your countertop, and flip the corresponding card over as you complete each task. When all the cards have been done, put them back behind their divider. You may choose to (or have to) finish some of the jobs when you return from work. Still, try to get all the Daily DO cards done every day.

Daily Chores cards. When you get home at night (and depending on your weariness, pressures, and other commitments), begin doing the

Daily Chores cards. You might not get through all of them, but when you have completed one card's task, put the card behind the others of the same type. Sometimes you will get all the Daily Chores cards done in one day, and sometimes it might take two or three days. The point is that you do them numerically so chores and responsibilities are approached with a semblance of order.

Wash DO cards. Each time you approach your wash, use the Wash DO cards to keep up on regular washing needs. The Wash Chores cards will help you to know which type of wash you will be doing next for items that need attention less often. This gets the wash done in an orderly manner even if it takes several weeks to get through the different "specialty" loads.

Weekly DO cards. There are also Weekly DO cards. These would best be done each week, but approach the cards' jobs in order, putting the card in the rear of the appropriate section in the index card box as you finish a job. This keeps these jobs done in a consistent, repetitive order, even if it takes several weeks to complete all the cards.

Weekly Chores cards. Each week as you approach housework (whether you do it, your family participates, or you pay someone to do it), you will want to use the Weekly Chores cards. As stated before, these jobs have been broken down into simple tasks that can be done here and there, such as just before leaving for work or between fixing dinner and going off to a meeting. Again, you pull the first card, finish the job, and put the card in the back of the appropriate section. This helps you approach the housework in an orderly manner, whether it all gets done each week (as you might like) or it takes two or three weeks to complete.

Monthly DO cards. Each month you have Monthly DO jobs as stated on your new housecleaning cards. Try to schedule these jobs on your planner or calendar. You will work best if these jobs are approached and finished each month. But again, do them in order, and when you have finished a chore, put the card in the back of the appropriate section. Then do the job listed on the next card behind the Monthly DO divider.

Monthly Chores cards. The Monthly Chores cards are less important monthly jobs and are approached after the Monthly DO card jobs are done. Again, finish a job, put the card in the back of the appropriate section of the index card box, and pull the card right behind the divider when you are able to do another job.

Some chores need to be approached according to the seasons of the year. These cards are kept behind different months according to the listing on each card divider. Sometimes you will be able to do these jobs in a timely manner, and sometimes they will have to wait. Sometimes they will be completely neglected, but the system allows you to be aware and connected with seasonal responsibilities.

LEARN HOUSECLEANING METHODS

Knowing the best way to clean a house will save time again and again. As indicated before, there are three basic kinds of cleaning: neatening (usually done every day), light cleaning (usually done between once a day and once a week), and deep cleaning (done less often, usually monthly, semiannually, or annually). This is one skill worth practicing with ruthless focus.

Housecleaning methods: Neatening. Neatening is NOT really cleaning at all, but it gives the illusion of cleanliness. Neatening is making the home look clean by picking things up and putting them away. A good way to accomplish this daily task is to acquire a cobbler's apron with two large pockets. The left pocket is for smaller items that are misplaced and need to be put in their rightful "home." The right pocket is for "garbage" items, which can be deposited in a wastebasket.

For a stay-at-home manager, after breakfast is done and your spouse and kids have left for work and school, put on that apron and go to work. You begin at the front door because that's the place you want to be the neatest, and you work around the house from there. Pick up items to keep and put them in the left pocket; deposit trash in the right pocket. Large objects that are out of place will have to be carried to their rightful home, but small items can be put in your apron. Straighten pillows, open curtains, put magazines away, collect empty soda cans, and make each room look as best as you can with this first "sweep through."

Bedrooms. When you get to the bedrooms, make the beds (if you haven't already taught your children to do that before they go to school), pick up stray items and deposit them in their homes, open the curtains, and shut the closet doors.

Bathroom. When you get to the bathroom, straighten items on the counter, close and flush the toilet, straighten the towels on their racks, pick up stray items, and straighten the rug. Leave the room looking as neat as you can. Do the same kinds of chores with your master and half bathrooms. There is no deep cleaning, just neatening or what you might also call "light cleaning."

Master bedroom. In your own bedroom, do the same maintenance routine: make the bed, open curtains, pick up and hang stray clothes, and straighten items on top of your dresser.

Kitchen. Clear off the table, get the dishes washed or in the dishwasher, close all the cupboard doors, wipe off the countertops (this must be done to make the kitchen look neat), and push in the chairs around the table.

Now walk around the house one more time to make sure that your "neatening" is done. Most spouses, children, or company do not readily see dirt and grime. They are more aware of the neatness of your home. In the same way, you will find that a neat home will be nicer to live in and easier to clean when you tackle those weekly and deeper cleaning jobs. The most important part of housework is picking up. In a matter of minutes you can have that done each morning and have a pristine "castle" to live in the rest of the day.

Housecleaning methods: Cleaning. Weekly cleaning chores are done with more attention paid to actually cleaning the rooms. Each room might have a list of specific cleaning standards to enable all family members to know when the job is complete. For example, cleaning a bathroom entails the following:

- Gathering up and shaking the rugs
- Wiping down the mirror
- Cleaning the counter and surround
- Wiping out the sink
- Cleaning the top of the towel racks and toilet tank top
- Cleaning the shower or bath
- Wiping down the shower surround or bath tile
- Sweeping the floor
- Mopping the floor
- Emptying the wastebasket

Housecleaning methods: Deep cleaning. Deep-cleaning jobs need specific standards and written instructions. For example, for convenience, instructions for changing furnace filters can be posted both on the kitchen wall and on the wall of the furnace room. Changing furnace filters means doing the following:

- Purchase appropriately sized furnace filters
- Remove panel from furnace
- Remove old furnace filters
- Insert new furnace filters
- Replace panel on furnace
- Discard old furnace filters

Tackling housecleaning and home-maintenance chores in a systematic way gives structure to the days and weeks of a family's life. It also provides a sense that "your work is done for the day" and that you can leave off housework and home maintenance if you have finished your list of chores. It is a time-saving way to move from haphazard to habitual living.

— » 4 « —

MADNESS
TO METHOD

Gain skills to
act more poised
than you
sometimes feel.

- *Action project:* Purge and organize the master bedroom and the master bedroom closet
- Maintain 22-tie rule (if one comes in, another goes out)
- Finish one season; prepare for the next
- Prepare before
- Gain momentum in four easy steps

In this chapter, you will focus on moving from madness to more methodical approaches to purging and organizing. As you continue to incorporate organization skills into your routines, the benefits of getting the master bedroom neat and orderly cannot be overemphasized. This is done by purging and organizing that room, employing essential organizational systems, and maintaining organization with a routine that works for you. This will reduce stress and increase your capacity to function at a higher level.

PURGE AND ORGANIZE THE MASTER BEDROOM AND MASTER BEDROOM CLOSET

Tackling your master bedroom closet is a great place to practice your newly learned organization skills because you probably have strong opinions about what is useful and needed, what is useful but not needed, and what is not useful and not needed. And having a purged closet will make a considerable improvement in your daily functioning.

Tackle your closet in three sections: hanging clothes, items on the floor, and items on the shelves. Start with your hanging clothes.

Master bedroom closet: Tools. The tools needed for purging the master bedroom closet are boxes (each labeled with the names of the other rooms in the house), white garbage bags, black garbage bags, a wastebasket, and a sufficient number of plastic hangers that are consistent in shape and size.

Take all the items off the hanging rods and place them on your bed (which should be made so you have a large, flat surface to work on). Sort the items four ways, putting them back in your closet or into your bags, boxes, and containers as you go.

- **Useful and needed items** go back in the closet or in the boxes to be stored elsewhere. Useful and needed items are clothes that you love, wear often, and would not want to go without.
- **Useful and not needed clothing** goes in white bags for sharing with charity or others. These are clothes that no longer fit, are out of style, are the wrong color, or are simply ones you don't like.
- **Not useful and not needed clothing** goes in black bags for discarding. These are items that should have been discarded before but now get the final shove out of your closet.
- **Some items are "maybes."** These items might fit again, you might eventually find another matching piece, or you might wear them occasionally. These items go in the rear of your closet, covered with a large towel, so they are available but are separated

from the rest. After six months, items still under the towel are ready to be shipped off to charity.

Remember that to have fewer clothes is to be less burdened by life. Generously rid yourself of all clothes that you really, really don't like. You will never miss them. Your closet will seem much larger. Dressing will become much easier, and you will feel much better about yourself.

There are two exceptions to this rule: seasonal and maternity clothing. Sort through these items before storing. Then they will be most useful when they are needed again.

The same system and routine will apply to purging and organizing your closet floor and shelving. Go through the items on your closet floor and your shelves. Strive to have more than enough room in your closet. It is not likely you will have more closet space anytime soon. So eliminate and simplify. It feels great!

KEY CONCEPT: When you set up a pattern for doing projects and then return to that same pattern again and again, you are organizing yourself to move the process to the back of your mind. With practice, you can organize easily and quickly because you have set up consistent tools, systems, and routines. The enchantment is not in using garbage bags of a certain color in a certain way, but in developing consistent organization tools, systems, and routines that translate into better control of your surroundings. This repetitive process helps you order your world with speed and efficiency.

MAINTAIN 22-TIE RULE (IF ONE COMES IN, ANOTHER GOES OUT)

The 22-tie rule is a fun way to remember to regularly purge. For example, a professional man usually dresses up (including a tie) twenty-two days each month. If he wears a different tie each workday of the month, he doesn't need more than twenty-two ties. Thus, if he adds a new tie to his collection and wants to maintain the status quo, he will give up one tie to charity or a local thrift store.

Shed before holidays and birthdays. This same concept can be used to help maintain a good balance of possessions in the home, especially during birthdays and holidays, when there tends to be an influx of possessions. Again, the best kind of shedding and sharing comes from giving away what is useful but no longer needed. Even after initially purging half of all your possessions, this continued shedding can be done proactively, energetically, and with a cheerful heart in the days before significant holidays and celebrations. It doesn't matter if you are giving the items to the local homeless shelter or taking your stash to a thrift store. Before birthdays and holidays, gather from your home what you don't need, pack it up, and get it gone. Soon enough, gifts will fill the empty space.

Every shirt in the give-away pile means that one more child will be clothed; every pair of shoes means that someone will have covered feet. Every unused and still-viable toy, game, and stuffed animal will get a chance to be loved by another family.

How do you do this? Start with a short family meeting and explain that you and your spouse have several large white garbage bags you hope will be completely filled with the "extras" from your home. Suggest a specific hour on Saturday morning when the family can work together to fill the bags with the surplus of your life. Remember, white bags reduce second-guessing because you can't easily see what you have contributed!

After shedding what is not needed in your life, those items will likely flow back to you if and when you need them again. So shed freely: the old jewelry, the pants that are attractive but hang unused in the closet after the first master bedroom purge, the three coats you have had for ten years but have only worn once or twice and haven't had the courage to give up because they were expensive.

You may never see the tears in the eyes of the recipients of your generosity, but you can imagine the joy of a good, clean piece of clothing warming both the heart and the soul of another. You can imagine the joy when the dusty toys of your storage areas take on new shine as they enliven the days of forlorn children.

Most of you don't live close to poverty, hunger, and despair. Life has been gracious. So let's shed and share with vigor. Several large white garbage bags filled with the extra, unneeded items from your home will provide plenty of surpluses for others' needs—and all without impinging on you and yours.

You're likely not to miss the items much. You will feel leaner and cleaner. It is inevitable that you and yours will gain more possessions during upcoming birthdays and holidays. So take a leap—and shed and share what you don't need!

Another time during the year when you can apply the 22-tie rule is when you are changing out seasonal clothing.

Manage seasonal clothing. Old Man Weather can fool you, especially during the transitions between seasons. He produces a sharply bitter day that sends you scurrying for warmer clothes and then laughs at you with several days or weeks of warm weather. Sometimes the weather turns chilly, and yet there are still occasional summertime temperatures during the day. How do you deal with this confusion?

Keep some long-sleeved shirts, light jackets, and sweaters hanging in your closet all year. These will get you through the chillier days and can be easily worn over other clothing. Children should also have a light jacket or sweater for school and play to keep them warm during these transition days.

Heavier and lighter seasonal clothing (usually winter and summer) should be stored separately. This means that you keep out lighter clothing during spring and summer, when your winter clothing is stored. Depending on your location, you should have a general idea when it is time to get the winter clothing out and put away the summer clothing.

When the weather has turned colder (usually when the first winter storms come to your area), open the containers with your winter clothes, lay the clothes on your bed, and sort through them. You may be surprised to find a few items that you can discard or give away. Do so! Then gather up your summer clothes and review whether they are useful and will be needed when it warms up again. If not, share them with charity. If you'll need them again, pack them neatly in the empty containers.

Hang up the winter clothes in your closet. Don't store the containers just yet, because there will inevitably be a stray item or two that will turn up in the next week or so. Besides, you may need to retrieve an item from the containers for a particularly warm day.

Pull out the winter clothes containers for your children, sort through them, and hang the clothes up—except for those clothes you are giving away. Gather up their summer clothes and return them to the empty containers, setting aside items that no longer fit, that wouldn't be suitable to use again, or that should be given away. Remember, whenever you do this "transition" project, always sort and simplify wherever possible—all with the goal of living a bit lean.

FINISH ONE SEASON; PREPARE FOR THE NEXT

In addition to ordering your seasonal wardrobe, it is prudent to also make an orderly transition from one season to the next. This is usually done about two weeks before the end of each season. For example, in families with children in school, the winter holidays give way to school pressures in January, school gives way to summertime relaxation (in traditional schools), summer gives way to school again, and then the year-end holidays descend, bringing children and teenagers home again.

The transition from summer to school is an example of how to finish one season and prepare for the next. Because the summer season seems to end too soon and school often descends before you are ready, many of your routines are in "overlap" during the last month of summer and the first month of school. You don't want to "finish" the season because it's still hot and it still feels like summer, and yet you must face the requirements of children's and teenagers' clothing, school supplies, and homework. How do you handle this overlap period and gain the cooperation of your family members to help put away one season even as you gear up and engage in the next?

Make an "overlap" list. Fold a piece of lined paper in half lengthwise and write "Finish Summer" on the top left and "Begin School" on the top right. Down the left side of the paper, list the items that still need attention to complete your family's summer projects, put away summer wardrobes, and store summertime toys and tools. Then, on the right side of the paper, list those items that need to be addressed to get ready for school/autumn. Finally, make pencil notations to indicate the family member responsible for initiating each of the projects.

Put the list on your refrigerator and add to it as you remember additional items. Having the list on the refrigerator will also bring it to the attention of your family members and help them want to add to it. You can also anticipate eliciting their cooperation by this subtle introduction to the projects. Soon your list will be sufficiently complete to discuss formally with the family at dinnertime.

KEY CONCEPT: Remember, to share responsibility is to let others contribute to the successful running of your home. You should invite each member of your family to take a lead role in at least one project. You will then gain the opportunity to emotionally bond and you will find that cooperative enthusiasm may increase.

Some of you are on a year-round school schedule, but even so, finishing summer and beginning fall will "happen" and thus still needs your attention. If you want to get, be, and stay organized, you would be wise to think about this concept as you move from season to season.

Personalize the overlap list. On the "Finish Summer" sublist, your "Seasonal Overlap" list might include three evenings for harvesting and freezing fruit from your garden, having another evening for a final picnic in a scenic locale, and mending three summer tops before storing them.

Your "Begin School" sublist might include finding online Spanish instruction (to help your teenager with a difficult language class during the upcoming school months), buying warmer socks because where you live it often snows by the end of the month, and taking advantage of end-of-summer school supply sales because you are low on binders, pencils, and glue.

Thinking through your needs, making a written list, and integrating these goals into your regular routines during the beginning of August will make the "overlap" season happen with greater ease.

Label what you store. (As you store summer items, consider using the system detailed in chapter 11.) Remembering where you stored things is much easier when you have reminders. For example, indicate on your online calendar when you want to check inner tubes for leaks before summer vacations start up again. In your planner, note where in the attic you put the blowup boat and life jackets. Put an entry on your shopping list about whose sandals you need to replace because they were lost or ruined.

KEY CONCEPT: The mind is not for remembering—paper, computers, and phones are. And this is especially true if your family is young, your family is large, or your schedule is complex.

Try to finish your summer projects, put away your summer toys and tools, and clean up your summer wardrobes by the middle of September. This lets your family settle into school-time routines without summer-time distractions.

And another list too. Even as you work with your "Finish Summer" and "Overlap" lists, begin an "Autumn To Do" list. This list could detail the many projects you want to complete before the holidays are upon you. There are usually eight precious weeks between September 1 and October 31. Somehow, in the period between when November begins and January is half done, you can't do much more than handle holiday pressures. But once your "Overlap" list is complete, priorities for these eight "Autumn" weeks will provide good directions for the next steps in your life.

If you have prepared for this seasonal transition, you'll be ahead (at least in theory) as you approach a new scholarly season. In the same way, you can plan for successful transitions between autumn and the winter holidays, between the winter holidays and the return to normal new-year routines, between winter and spring, and, going around the calendar again, between spring and summer.

PREPARE BEFORE

Learning to be ahead of the game saves significant time and trouble. When you are not rushed and stressed, you make more logical, thoughtful decisions. Thus the concept of "preparing before." Whenever you practice preparing before stress goes up, you are going to come out ahead. Let's look at potential ways to practice this principle.

Prepare for your week the day before. If Monday morning goes really well, the rest of the week seems to go just as well. But you may find that you struggle with getting your week off to a good start. Of course, in your mind, you are going to get everything done (everything that's important and essential for the week) as soon as possible. But the day (and sometimes the whole week) can seem to fall apart when the week starts with an unavoidable repair, unexpected interruption, or just one or two things out of routine.

So how do you conquer the challenges that you face every Monday morning? Five skills help relieve stress, dampen depression, and keep you going.

1. **Make a list.** More than any other stress reliever, making a list of what needs your attention is essential to your success. This is a list above and beyond your regular housecleaning and home-maintenance chores. This list will sometimes be frustratingly long. No matter, write everything down that needs your attention.

KEY CONCEPT: To give you regular direction and focus, begin making this list at the end of the week for the next week's priorities. It is easier to change a list than to create it, so during the weekend, get your stresses, projects, and problems down on paper as a first step toward having a better week.

2. **Set priorities.** Weigh each item on your list according to importance. Use the ABC system. If it is essential, it gets an "A." If it is important, it gets a "B." If it would be nice to have done, it gets a "C."

3. **Schedule your priorities!** With your revised, prioritized list in hand, review the scheduling needs the week will present you. Decide which day and time you would best address each "A" item. When you are running errands on Thursday, could you add two "A" items to your list and make just one trip? Can you read that "A" article while you wait during your children's piano lessons on Wednesday? Can you have someone help with that "A" repair on Saturday morning (after your family has had a good, hot breakfast together)?

   Add "B" items to each day's schedule, to be done only if time allows. Put the "C" items at the bottom of your daily schedule, to be tackled only if plenty of extra time allows or someone kindly asks how he or she can help. In other words, first focus on your regular weekly responsibilities, then work on the "As," then the "Bs," and sometimes the "Cs." Remember, always do the most important things first.

(This procedure differs from those described in chapter 6 and chapter 12. Here, you are learning how to use a to-do list to prepare before. In chapter 6, you will learn how to apply this to-do list concept during times of stress and change. In chapter 12, you will learn how to better work through emotional needs using another type of list.)

4. **Leave time for the inevitable.** Sometimes, just as you have everything set and ready to go, you will climb into your vehicle and find you are out of gas. Such challenges are distressing, but every day for the rest of your life will probably have some challenge, some repair, or some problem to be solved. Plan for it. Schedule it in. (Of course, keep a "B" and a "C" item or two ready to slip into those spare minutes should you have a really, really smooth day.)

5. **Stop and rest before you run out of energy.** You can work and work until you are past weariness. This is not wise! It makes you cranky, sometimes means a burnt dinner, and often means an unhappy family (funny how they seem to act just about as happy as you are). Listen to your body and stop before you run out of energy. Take a few minutes to regroup and rest. If you don't, it takes much longer to renew yourself enough to finish out the day.

List, then prioritize, then schedule. Plan time for inevitable interruptions and track your energy level. Monday mornings are going to come every week. Plan first and then go to work, keeping a smile on your face and that ABC list close at hand.

Prepare for your morning the night before. Having a method that reduces and eliminates confusion is especially applicable to morning routines. Morning is not the time to make decisions, prepare for the day, or finalize plans. All of that should happen the night before. Mornings are for getting ready, eating, and getting out the door. So how can you have better mornings?

- **Decide before.** Decide the night before what you will wear the next day. Decide when you need to set the alarm clock. Decide what you will have for breakfast. Decide how to tackle your morning chores so that if something has to wait until later, you will have done the most essential items first.

- **Establish children's nightly routines.** Children's nightly routines could include picking out their clothes for the next day so there is less emotional upheaval the next morning. Place lunch containers on the kitchen counter and help children put all non-refrigerated items in their lunch bag, with cold items conveniently stored in the refrigerator for retrieval in the morning. Make sure all folders, books, permission slips, and any signed paperwork are already tucked away in backpacks. Children will see what is needed to get them out the door in the morning and will learn the key organization tool of "prepare before." All these activities can happen without the time stresses mornings bring.

- **Inform the night before.** Does everyone in the family know what is happening tomorrow? When will Mom be home? When and where will Dad be picking the children up for piano lessons? What special chores need attention before the children can play with their friends?

KEY CONCEPT: Your family members don't like being in the dark when it comes to scheduling. Coordinate the best you can by discussing the next day's plans at tonight's dinner table. Make sure that everyone knows exactly what to expect, when to expect it, and how to respond if things don't go quite as planned.

If things aren't going smoothly for you, try a simple change to these "prepare before" routines and see how much it helps. Make decisions the night before, prepare the night before, and inform everyone of plans the night before. It will make a tremendous difference in the madness, stress, and tension of your mornings.

Prepare for the day each morning. For the stay-at-home parent, mornings often bring states of disorder and disarray that need to be addressed for there to be a smoother day. So why not prepare for the day as part of your morning routines?

- **Weekday mornings.** You can set an example by making your own bed, getting dressed, and organizing the contents in your master bedroom. You can fix breakfast for the youngest children and then eat too. Older, able-bodied members of the family can fix their own breakfast on weekdays.

Then, once you are ready for your weekday, encourage your older children to prepare for their days before they leave for school. Make a written, laminated list of what needs to be done to get ready for school. Hang this list in your children's bedroom or bathroom. For those who don't read, you can use pictures (either photos of them doing the activity or simple graphics) to guide them:

» Get dressed
» Make bed
» Eat breakfast
» Brush teeth
» Comb hair
» Do morning job
» Get backpack and lunch container

Using this method will teach them accountability for their personal responsibilities and also suggest an order for completing their personal tasks.

With preschoolers, you might put simple words and graphics on 3" x 5" cards. Punch the cards in one corner and string them together with a metal binder ring. The cards might list some or all of the following morning chores:

» Get hug and kiss from someone
» Make my bed
» Straighten my room
» Hang up my clothes
» Get dressed
» Put on shoes
» Put my pajamas away
» Wash my face
» Comb my hair
» Eat breakfast
» Put my breakfast dishes in the sink
» Brush my teeth
» Serve someone

Look carefully at the morning routines of your family. It is in the simplest of habits, in the regularity of routines, and in the consistent insistence on a week-to-week basis that you lay the foundation for order in your family members' lives.

- **Weekend mornings.** On the weekends, you can also persuade children to get ready for the day before they engage in video games, play with their friends, or start personal projects. Every child, teenager, and adult should practice core activities to "get ready for the weekend." These simple but repetitive habits will lay a solid foundation both for you and for your children, even in the luxury and leisure of weekend days.

Family members should do the following:

- » Get dressed
- » Make their beds
- » Put pajamas away
- » Straighten up their rooms
- » Eat breakfast
- » Brush their teeth

Even young children can help with these weekend activities. For example, they can place their pillow on their bed made by an older sibling or parent. Young children can place their pajamas in the designated place. For breakfast, they can get out a bowl for cold cereal, put their bowl and spoon in the sink after they eat, and brush their teeth as their way of helping out.

Teach your family to get themselves ready for their weekdays and their weekends. Then, once their chores are also done, they can indulge in the more pleasurable weekday and weekend routines.

Prepare for tomorrow today. When children arrive home from school, ensure they have a designated landing spot for their backpack and another for their lunch container. Then have them help you empty out the contents of both. Use a simple folder system to help children put their homework and other papers back in the right place in their backpack once their homework is done. This makes for easier retrieval when it is time to pass their homework in. For elementary children, the folders might be labeled "Spelling Words," "Math," "Reading," or "For

Teacher." This will help children organize their papers in the relaxation and safety of their home.

Also have a homework center with a caddy full of school supplies that are easily available to the children. The homework center may be a personal bedroom desk or the kitchen table, where they will gather to do their homework under your supervision. Establishing school-day routines, especially when children are young, will guide them as to what is expected of them to prepare for tomorrow today. It also teaches accountability for their responsibilities before and after school.

Help your children be responsible all the way to the end of their days as a major step toward personal motivation and self-initiative for tomorrow's needs.

GAIN MOMENTUM IN FOUR EASY STEPS

Sometimes it is hard to get started on the next project, such as today's laundry or last night's dishes. As you become more organized, engage in momentum-gaining activities. Here are several steps that will help ensure self-motivation success:

- **Visual reminders.** Use visual reminders to remind you of your goals and to keep you on track. Sadly, you can get easily distracted in the midst of everyday responsibilities. For example, if you struggle to get a batch of laundry going in the morning, create a sign for your bathroom mirror that says, "LAUNDRY FIRST."
- **A timer.** Use a timer to kick-start your engagement in a menial task. You will likely find it's easier to begin a task if you have an ending time you can anticipate. Starting is often the hardest part, but pushing through becomes easier if you mentally commit to staying with your task for the fifteen minutes set on the timer.
- **If-Then.** Have a specific If-Then response to help remind you of your commitments. (Nothing like a game to keep you interested.) For example, "If I get the laundry going, then I'll have some breakfast."

- **Tell a trusted friend.** Tell someone important to you (and who you trust not to make fun of your "bad" days) about your goals and encourage their involvement in your change. For example, you might tell your spouse that for the next week you are going to work on getting the laundry done and put away in a timely manner. Then report at dinnertime about your progress.

Pick one organization item that needs focus in your personal life and resolve on these four momentum-gaining steps of success. Write up reminder notes. Use a timer. Decide on an If-Then response. Get someone to encourage and prompt you on your way. Soon your laundry will be done, or you will be exercising every day, or you will be getting dressed first thing in the morning. These small but important organization skills can become firm habits to enhance your life.

— » 5 « —

RUSHED TO RELAXED

Keep life
under control,
paperwork filed,
and information
retrievable.

- **Action project:** Purge and organize the home office
- Find paperwork in thirty seconds or less
- Keep family journals
- Think with your brain; remember with your hand
- Use permanent lists
- Do what's important before it becomes urgent

This chapter will first focus on purging and organizing the home office. Then the focus will move toward having a workable filing system, setting up permanent lists to facilitate repeated ventures, and tackling projects before they become urgent. Remember, when you want to be more organized, you plan outward from handling things "just for now" to handling items "always and forever."

PURGE AND ORGANIZE THE HOME OFFICE

As you gain expertise purging the other rooms in your home, consider the special needs of your home office or home office area. If this area has fallen into disarray, you may need several hours or several partial days to purge it of unnecessary clutter and set it up for usefulness again.

Initially, clear off and clean out all unneeded items in the home office. Put items that are useful and needed—but that might be stored elsewhere—in your previously prepared and labeled boxes. Put items to share in white garbage bags and items to be tossed in black garbage bags. Papers that need special handling can be put in white garbage bags, labeled "need to shred," and set aside for this type of disposal.

If you have bookcases, their contents should be attractive to the eye, meet your office needs, and complement the complete organized look you are trying to achieve. Purge what doesn't belong, is obsolete, or should be stored elsewhere. Wipe down all flat surfaces and office furniture.

Now it is time to set up the home office so it's more effective for your daily use.

KEY CONCEPT: Start at your office door and work around the room counter-clockwise (if you are right-handed) and clockwise (if you are left-handed). Start at the top shelf/drawer/cupboard and work down and then across and around the room. This directional purging will take advantage of the circular motion of your dominant arm while speeding up your progress.

You can use this same pattern when cleaning the house, washing the car, or cleaning windows. Right-handed people work counter-clockwise around the project. Left-handed people work clockwise.

Paperwork storage. If you have paperwork that must be kept for several years or indefinitely, but you don't have room in your office to do so, plan to store this paperwork in a more out-of-the-way place in your home or garage. Buy or find a dozen or so filing or moving boxes (usually available at office supply stores). You will also need one hundred or more manila file folders. It is also helpful to have several large black garbage bags for discarding obsolete paperwork, magazines, and newspapers that don't need shredding. These papers will be thrown out at the end of your purging sessions. (During the purging process, be more ruthless than generous. If you don't absolutely need it, toss it.)

Label the boxes with the general categories of paperwork in your office. For example: **Current Files—2018** (paperwork that needs to be saved for now), **Can Discard—December 2020** (these papers will eventually be thrown out), **Save Until—January 2025** (and then discard if unneeded), or **Store Permanently**, and **Don't Know**. As you fill one box with paperwork, add "#1" after its title. For example, **Can Discard— December 2020, Box #1**. Then begin box #2 with the same labeling and continue to work.

Financial paperwork. If you don't own a business, save personal financial/tax/business papers for ten years. This ten-year timing is easier to remember than the currently required seven years. For example, if you come upon personal financial paperwork that isn't useful for tax deductions and is older than 2010, you can throw this financial paperwork out in 2020.

All business-related paperwork is best saved for lengthier periods of time, according to the advice of your financial advisor. If you are working for a home-based company and thus coping with company paperwork, you need to find out their policy for saving paperwork and act accordingly.

(Note that storing this type of paperwork long-term uses a different method than the general storage system detailed in chapter 11. It also differs from the specific labeling system for storing clothing, as mentioned in chapter 13.)

Go to work. Pick up a piece of paper, or a stack of papers, and decide if and where to store them. Prepare a new, labeled folder, if necessary. Put papers in this folder in the proper storage box. You must be decisive and move forward, even if you change your mind as you continue to work. Being decisive is a skill an organized person practices regularly. Move ahead with reasonable speed and confidence!

Set a timer and focus on purging and organizing your home office for thirty minutes, and then take a five-minute rest and bathroom break. Go back to work for another thirty minutes. Bring into the room a lunch or snack and eat during one of these breaks, taking fifteen or so minutes. Then go back to work. Keeping at the task will help you have focus, gain confidence, and maintain reasonable progress. Set aside this project when other priorities press upon you, but plan to come back tomorrow or very soon. A cleaned-out and organized home office is a vital part of functioning at a highly organized level.

Knowing that you will have to use your creative juices to apply these activities to your current situation, let's look at the important elements of an effective home office. The three main essentials are: a flat surface (the bigger the better), a small drawer for office supplies and paperwork tools, and a larger drawer for filing papers.

Flat surface. While an actual desk with small drawers for office supplies and large drawers for filing is optimal, get creative with your current situation. For those without an official home office, other useful flat surfaces may include a kitchen table or a smaller table in a corner of the master bedroom. But two things are very important.

Your desk is meant to be an "A" space. This means that most items put there are used on a regular basis and can be reached while sitting. It is not meant to be a storage area. Keep what you use most often closer at hand and move lesser-used items to lesser-used areas of the office.

Keep the desk surface reasonably clear at all times—unless there is a project at hand. This is because most paperwork is best handled without first having to clean up a previous mess. This clean, flat surface is maintained by finishing your current project and putting it away before you leave your desk and go to other tasks.

Or keep one small drawer as a "landing" place for partially finished projects that you plan to come back to later. This keeps the desk surface clean and ready.

Office supplies drawer/container. Designate a small drawer for office supplies. In some cases, this will be a container that you keep near you when doing paperwork, especially if your desk doesn't have drawers or you are using another flat surface for your duties. Gather or purchase tools that will help you handle paperwork: paper clips, a stapler, a three-hole punch, pencils and pens, sticky notes, and tape. Keep these together and close to the "desk," so when you sit down you can go right to work. If you have to stand or move around to retrieve a tool, you are more likely to become distracted and not complete the task at hand.

To facilitate this process, label tools "home office" or purchase ones of similar colors. There should also be extra scissors, pens, and pencils that can be borrowed from the home office by members of the household.

File folders drawer/container. Clean out a deep drawer or box to hold file folders. Then put essential paperwork there to facilitate retrieval with a minimum of hassle.

Label these file folders to meet personal needs:

- **Auto insurance**
- **Home insurance**
- **Medical insurance**
- **Pay stubs**
- **Receipts** for _____ (list year)
- **Taxes** for _____ (list year)
- **Vital documents**. Copies of important documents such as birth certificates, Social Security cards, marriage certificates, trusts, wills, end-of-life paperwork, and adoption papers. The actual documents are best kept in a safe-deposit box or fireproof safe.

Keep similar documents together in appropriately labeled folders. It is not always convenient to file paperwork right away, but it is a useful habit for saving time when you need that paperwork again. Other topical or alphabetical filing folders can be added depending on the needs of your household. These might include an alphabetical filing system for keeping instructions and warranties or an alphabetical filing system for keeping interesting articles regarding a spouse's hobby.

So look at your situation and go to work. Find a flat surface to call your desk, whether it be a card table you set up in the corner of the family room or your bedroom, a real desk that has been previously covered with another's papers, books, and magazines, or your own desk after finally cleaning it off. Gather or purchase office tools to meet your home-office needs. Label them and do whatever else is necessary to make sure they stay where they belong. Prepare a box or larger drawer for your file folders and store your needed paperwork there.

It will take several hours of hard, dedicated work to clean out and clean up your home office. By the end, you are likely to have several bags of papers that need to be shredded or discarded, several boxes of paperwork that need to be deep-stored, and several boxes of personal items that can be stored elsewhere.

The goal is to have your office look professional. This means it is neat, lean on clutter, and easy to work in. A functional home-office haven can be yours as you continue your pursuit of personal organization. Fix it up and then keep it up. What a great investment in your future competency. A revived office means a better, smoother-running home!

Keep desktop cleared. The biggest challenge entails keeping the desktop cleared (unless you are working on a project), keeping your desk tools where they belong, and using the labeled file folders to aid in your home-office organization. With time, you will find that having a home office will aid you greatly with planning each day, calendaring, planning your housework, preparing menus, dealing with the trivia of life, and planning for bulk-food and sundries purchases.

Begin the process of gaining control of your paperwork and you will step closer to being a professional home manager with your own functioning home office!

File paperwork immediately. After you have set up your home office to your liking, practice handling your paperwork flow. This habit is vital to having your office remain the haven you have worked so hard to create. While it is not always possible to tackle this need every day, realize that a paper that is piled is lost, while one that is filed is found. It is always easier and faster to deal with a few pieces of paper now than to wait until the mess delays your finding the paperwork you need. Regular home-office maintenance is part of the process of staying organized.

FIND PAPERWORK IN THIRTY SECONDS OR LESS

After you have established your home office for keeping long-term paperwork filed conveniently, you are ready to organize paperwork that regularly moves in and out of your life. This includes mail, magazines, and school work.

Keep three tools convenient to the home office area and employ skills that make "rotating" paperwork retrieval easy and convenient. A fourth tool, a teenager filing system, is kept in the teenager's bedroom.

These tools are:

- **In and out letter trays.** Have one labeled tray for every member of the family five years old and above.
- **A desktop filing system.** This is where family members can keep their "rotating" paperwork.
- **Family Information binder.** This binder is a place for every important reference piece of paper.
- **Teenager filing system.** This tool is used to teach teenagers the rudiments of filing and to move them toward self-reliant behavior patterns.

In and out letter trays. Stacked "in and out" plastic letter trays, which can be purchased from an office supply store, organize incoming mail and papers of all kinds. Labeled trays for each member of the family should be neatly stacked. Mom's tray usually goes on top because she tends to handle a larger portion of paperwork. School papers, mail, and other papers that come into the house can have an initial "home" where they can go. This immediately reduces the paper clutter so often found on the kitchen counters or the kitchen desk.

Desktop filing. It is difficult to keep track of reference paperwork that needs to be kept only temporarily and yet seems to disappear when needed most.

A desktop filing system will keep your home desk counter clean, your active life in place, and accommodate your fallible mind. As with all systems, once it is in place, the key is regularly looking in the files to find the relevant paperwork.

This detailed system works wonderfully, all while keeping the refrigerator door free of wedding invitations and flat surfaces clear of unpaid bills. This system also allows paperwork to move from your letter trays to a second, more organized "home" until you can address each need.

Desktop filing: Tools.

- One file folder holding container.
- Folder labeled **TO-DO**. Papers that need attention go here.
- Folder labeled **BILLS TO PAY**. Unpaid bills go here.
- Folder labeled **PENDING**. Papers that are halfway done, such as unanswered letters you initiated, or anything else that is in suspension goes here.
- Folder labeled **TO FILE**. Paperwork you are considering keeping goes here to season for a month or so before being added to your permanent files or discarded because interest has waned.
- Thirty-one folders, labeled **1–31** (for the days of the month). Bridal and baby shower invitations go here and are stored about one week before the event.
- Twelve folders, labeled **January–December**. Information about next year's reunion, upcoming community events, or to-do lists you will tackle later go here.
- One folder, labeled **Next Year.** Paperwork that needs to be kept but won't be managed for some time goes here.
- One folder, labeled **Master Grocery Lists**. Spare Master Grocery List forms (as explained more fully in chapter 7) will go here.

Set up a system for handling the presence of "too many" papers and relieve enormous stress in your life. Divide, confine, and conquer your paperwork to bring a great sense of control into your life. This will also help you think clearly and plan more efficiently. With these tools in place, you can now use a system to keep yourself "ahead of the game."

Desktop filing: System. When paperwork first enters the home, it should be put either in the letter trays or the desktop filing system. For example, when wedding and baby shower invitations are received, the date of the event goes on your calendar and the paperwork goes in a daily folder one week before the wedding or shower. This allows time for acquiring the gift, wrapping the gift, and arranging to attend.

Correspondence you are going to delay responding to might be stored under the next month's folder. An example of this is a letter you received but don't plan to reply to until you discuss the situation in person when your mother comes to visit next month.

Handwritten notes about bulbs and where they were planted in your garden can be put under March, conveniently available for knowing where to look for the shoots.

Keep notes of summer-activity ideas under the monthly folder titled June, along with information about local swimming lessons, summer-school opportunities, and coupons for getting discounted milkshakes. Use this filing method to keep ideas safe until you need them.

Desktop filing: Routine. Using the desktop filing system systematically and creatively will simplify your life even as it accommodates your many commitments.

Put paperwork into the letter trays or desktop filing system as it comes into your home. Retrieve paperwork each morning from the daily folders (those labeled 1–31). Address, discard, or refile the paperwork as appropriate. Using this method, you will never need to have "temporary" papers lying out in your home again.

Family Information binder. This binder will hold important information that you will likely refer to throughout the year. There are four major sections and several subsections in the binder:

- **Household Information**
- **Family Information**
- **Medical Information**
- **Prescription Information**

Household Information section. Purchase and label six binder dividers with the following:

- Numbers
- Purse/Wallet Contents
- Safe-Deposit Box
- Special Occasions
- Storage
- Keys

The **Numbers** sub-section is a place to store information regarding numbers you may need to refer to occasionally, including checking and savings account numbers, car insurance numbers, health insurance numbers, library card numbers, and passwords.

The **Purse/Wallet Contents** sub-section is a place to store a copy of the front and back of your purse or wallet contents. Such information is valuable if these items are ever lost or stolen.

The **Safe-Deposit Box** sub-section is a place to record the items in your safe-deposit box—if you use this method to keep original documents safe. It is useful to keep copies of these important documents in this section, too, for easy reference.

The **Special Occasions** sub-section is a permanent place to record birthday and holiday plans, preparations, and traditions. This helps you remember what you gave your nephew last year at Christmas and what his younger brother will likely be anticipating as a future gift.

The **Storage** sub-section is a place to make notes about larger items you have put into deeper storage, either at home or at a formal storage location.

Behind the **Keys** sub-section, put an 8½" x 11" clear plastic business card holder. Place a spare of each key you regularly use in an available space. Add a blank business card (or use the rear side of printed business cards) and write the purpose of the key. Tape the opening closed. These keys become  your personal "backup" keys. This key holder is kept at the back of the binder because it is heavier and somewhat bulky.

Family Information section. For the Family Information section, purchase and prepare additional binder dividers:

- **Labeled dividers** for each member of your family. For example, "Dad," "Mom," "Ted," and "Sue."

Put pertinent, current paperwork you will refer to often behind the appropriate dividers. For instance, John's soccer schedule will go behind his divider. Tom's piano recital schedule will go behind his divider.

KEY CONCEPT: You may also choose to have a family meeting where you impress everyone's fingerprints on a simple cardstock form, making additional notes about unique markings on each family member's body (moles, scars, and blemishes) and other comments that would help identify family members in case of an emergency. (See "Family Identification Form" in the appendix.) This information, along with current photos, would be invaluable if a disaster scattered the family.

FAMILY IDENTIFICATION FORM					
Last Name					
First Name					
Date					
	Thumb	1st Finger	2nd Finger	3rd Finger	4th Finger
Right Hand					
	4th Finger	3rd Finger	2nd Finger	1st Finger	Thumb
Left Hand					
Birthmarks					
Scars					
Moles					
Special Physical Traits					

Medical Information section. The **Medical Information** section is extremely important. You live in a mobile society. You may move. Your doctors and dentists may move or retire. Things change. If you keep good medical records, you won't spend endless hours tracking down essential medical information that was readily available at the time of your appointments. If you need more detailed information, you will know whom to call and how to reference the material you need. It only takes a few minutes to complete your notes, and you have a place to put important medical information you receive.

Purchase and prepare the following binder dividers:

- **Labeled dividers** for each member of your family. For example, "Dad—Medical," "Mom—Medical," "Ted—Medical," and "Sue—Medical."

- **Medical Information forms.** Behind these dividers, you may want to make up simple forms for keeping notes. You will need one form per person for doctors' visits and one for dental visits. Each of these sheets should have a place for Date, Doctor/ Dentist, and Reason for Visit. Other sheets can be prepared for immunizations, childhood diseases, and maternity records. Keep special medical instructions, county immunization cards, and other medical information in the appropriate places behind each person's divider.

Prescription Information section. Several needs are addressed when we store paperwork in this section: prescription receipts, the prescription information paperwork, your summary of the prescription dosage, timing, and purpose. In addition, keep an updated list of currently taken medication.

There are good reasons for the paperwork that comes with any prescription. It is wise to handle the paperwork that comes with prescriptions as soon as it comes into your home. There will probably be receipts that might help document a reduction to your taxes and also drug information to help you understand allergic reactions, the proper way to ingest the medication, and life-threatening possibilities. Also, you would be well advised to make summary notes for future reference.

So let's tackle this problem bit by bit until you have a simple system that works. Remember, whenever you get organized, you look at three needs: tools, systems, and routines. When you manage prescriptions, you will handle receipts, store prescription information, and make a short summary regarding the circumstances surrounding the prescription.

Prescription receipts: Tools. It will be useful to keep all prescription receipts for one year's time in one central location, usually the labeled file folder previously mentioned: **Receipts for ____.** This folder will also hold receipts for other purchases. This will make it convenient for finding receipts when you need them and for knowing where receipts are when you prepare your tax forms. It would be best to tape this folder on both ends to keep the smaller receipt slips from falling out the sides and getting lost.

Prescription receipts: System. Everyone has different systems (in other words, methods) for dealing with smaller pieces of paperwork, but you probably know three things about yourself: you tend to put paperwork down instead of putting it away, you tend to move your piles around without filing them, and you tend to lose a lot of paperwork, at least for the moment.

Thus, a good system is to always put prescription receipts in the correct folder instead of putting them down anywhere else.

Prescription receipts: Routine. Routines are the "when" of doing a project. When you rip the prescription receipt off the prescription sack, you will want to put it right away in the **Receipts for 2018** folder. Don't lay it down on the counter, set it on a paperwork pile, or lose it by setting it down carelessly somewhere else in the house.

Prescription information paperwork: Tools. The **Prescription Information** section of the Family Information binder should have labeled binder dividers:

- **Labeled divider: Unread Rx Information**
- **Labeled dividers** for each member of your family. For example, "Dad—Rx," "Mom—Rx," "Ted—Rx," and "Sue—Rx." These dividers can be kept behind the Prescription Information section of the Family Information binder.

Prescription information paperwork: System. A good system for handling drug paperwork is to take the papers out of the sack when you remove the prescription bottle, take a moment to peruse the paperwork, and then staple, three-hole punch, and confine the paperwork behind the proper family member's binder prescription divider.

Prescription information paperwork: Routine. The "when" of reading and filing prescription paperwork is a bit trickier. Many times, you don't have the time or the inclination to read the fine print right away. The children need dinner or the ill person needs medication, so you put this paperwork down with good intentions of reading it later.

Instead, consider putting prescription information paperwork down in the right place behind the **Prescriptions Information** divider you have labeled: **Unread Rx Information**. This way the paperwork is confined properly (so it won't get lost) and is designated as unread. After you have a chance to review this paperwork, it can be put behind the proper family member's divider.

Prescription summary: Tools. Use a simple form to summarize prescription information. (See "Prescriptions Summary Form" in the appendix.) For easy reference, these forms would be kept right

PRESCRIPTIONS SUMMARY FORM					
Date	Name	Doctor	Reason	Rx Number	Details

behind each individual's Prescription Information binder divider. The headers of this form would be as follows:

Date	Name	Doctor	Reason	Rx Number	Details

Prescription summary: System. When a prescription is brought home, the receipt is filed and the detailed paperwork confined. Six details are entered in the **Prescriptions Summary** form. To avoid confusion, note details on each person's summary form. The following is an example of a filled-out form:

Date	Name	Doctor	Reason	Rx Number	Details
October 2018	John	Dr. Shar	Warts on thumb near nail	#3342567	Apply liquid to wart 3 times/day for 2 weeks

Prescription summary: Routine. It is best to take a moment as soon as possible after arriving home to make these important notations. The situation is fresh in your mind and the bottle is often right in your hand.

Prescriptions currently taken: Tools. This form keeps track of current medications for family members with chronic health problems. (See "Prescriptions Currently Taken Form" in the appendix.) The headers for this form might have the following entries:

Reason	Date Begun	Date Ended	Doctor	Rx Name	Rx Dose/Frequency/ Directions

Prescriptions currently taken: System. This form has to be updated only when prescriptions are added or deleted.

Prescriptions currently taken: Routine. Take this **Prescriptions Currently Taken** form with you whenever you or the person involved sees a physician. Then all those participating in the well-being of your family member can have a clear and accurate understanding of prescription details.

Remember that taking prescriptions is meant to alleviate suffering, but it also means a responsibility to keep reasonable records. Use these systems and routines. Soon you will be confident and comfortable about saving prescription receipts, keeping documentation, and making summary notes. Your family members' prescription histories will be safe and you will be able to speak to any physician about the current prescriptions in your loved ones' lives.

	Date Begun	Date Ended	Doctor	Rx Name	Rx Dose/Frequency/ Directions
Reason					

PRESCRIPTIONS CURRENTLY TAKEN FORM

This type of organizing will be well worth your trouble. Oh, it feels good to have one more paperwork challenge under control!

Teenager filing systems. As your family members mature (usually around twelve to sixteen years of age), help them gain independence in handling their own personal paperwork. Relieve yourself of that responsibility and give them some paperwork-management practice while they are still under your guidance.

Teenage filing system: Tools. Purchase or find the following tools:

- **A sturdy plastic filing box with a lid.** While harder to find, it is better if the lid hinges have metal pins, the handle is not part of the lid, the box is large and sturdy (to reduce the possibility of tipping over), and the lid allows for storage of pens, labels, and paper clips.
- **20–25 Pendaflex file folders**
- **20–25 manila folders**
- **Blank file folder labels, marking pens, and scissors** (to keep in lid of container)

Teenage filing system: System. Label Pendaflex folders and manila folders according to your needs using similar labels for both folders. Other file folders can be added depending on the needs of your household. Suggestions for file labels include the following:

»	Pending	»	Photos
»	To File	»	Receipts
»	Church	»	School
»	Computer	»	Taxes
»	Finances	»	Vehicle
»	Friends	»	Vital Documents
»	Hobbies	»	Warranties
»	Job	»	Blanks (for
»	Journal items		personalization)
»	Passwords		

Teenage filing system: Routine. (1) Put papers in the "Pending" manila folder (which is kept inside the Pendaflex "Pending" folder). For example, keep an invitation here until the even thappens or keep a letter that has been written here until an answer is received. (2) Put papers in the "To File" manila folder to keep paperwork safe until the teenagers have time to file the paperwork. (3) File papers under other topics as soon as possible to keep them safe from loss, bending, or other ruin. (4) Retrieve papers as necessary. (5) When refilling, retain alphabetical order and put the manila folder back in the Pendaflex folder with the same label. This is another way to encourage independence and self-sufficiency in maturing young adults.

KEEP FAMILY JOURNALS

Just as some paperwork only needs a temporary home, some children's treasured paperwork, including homework, artwork, invitations, and programs, should be organized for permanent keeping. What should be kept and what should be discarded? How much is enough? Where and how should it be stored?

Family journals: Tools. Set up a simple, systemized way to deal with children's important papers. Soon after a child is born, purchase and prepare the following:

- **An 8½" x 11" binder.** Choose a different-colored binder for each member of your family.
- **Twenty dividers.** These are labeled with the year of birth and the succeeding nineteen years, for a total of twenty dividers.
- **A ream of 68-pound archival cardstock.** This cardstock is available at office supply stores. Three-hole punch a stack of the card stock and put it in the rear of the binder. Alternatively, store some of the card stock in a plastic sheet protector.
- **One hundred plastic sheet protectors.** Put about twenty-five of these plastic sheet protectors in the back of the binder.
- **An archival glue stick, photo mounting squares, and photo corners.** These tools are for mounting smaller items onto the cardstock.
- **A plastic binder pencil holder.** Keep the glue stick, photo mounting squares, and photo corners, along with a writing pen, in a three-hole binder pencil holder at the front of your binder. This makes for convenient updating of the journals. Now you are ready for easy journaling.

Family journals: System. When you decide a paper is worth keeping, three-hole punch it and put it in the binder behind the appropriate year's divider. Alternately, you can slip a treasured paper into a sheet protector you have stored in the back of the binder and put it in the binder behind the appropriate year's divider.

If a paper such as a newspaper article announcing the birth of your child is too small to punch and put in the binder, glue it to a piece of the cardstock stored at the back of the binder, write any comments you deem necessary with your writing pen, and place the cardstock in a sheet protector behind the appropriate divider in the child's binder. You can add other small items to this same sheet of cardstock. Some items, like certificates, might be better saved using photo corners. If you don't have a lot of time when a piece of paper needs to be stored, slip it into a plastic sheet protector and put it behind the appropriate divider until you have time to properly preserve it.

As one journal binder becomes full, purchase another of the same color. Put the remaining unused labeled dividers, spare cardstock, plastic sheet protectors, and other supplies into the new binder and you are ready for saving more family journal paperwork. For most children, six to eight binders will be enough to hold all their important "paper" journal items until they have finished high school. As they mature, they can enjoy looking back at their more rudimentary artwork and their simplistic handwriting.

Family journals: Routines. Most children's artwork and homework can safely be saved by punching and putting it in the binder. However, you need only so many original drawings to represent a child's artistic interests from a particular season of the child's life, so carefully select what you save. Children will bring home far more school paperwork that you will want to keep. Each school year, it is usually enough to keep a representative paper from each subject (usually their best work), creative art projects, and any papers with positive comments from the teacher. Be sure to save everything autobiographical that the child writes! It will become priceless as time passes.

Bigger school projects. School projects that are too large for keeping in these binders might best be displayed in the home for a month or so. Then, as the season for display wanes, take a picture of the child and their project, and then hold a "project" funeral. The photos can be saved in the children's journal. This plan excludes any items that might be reused for younger siblings' needs. Many a science project has seen an appropriate reuse to save parents' time and trouble.

Bulkier treasures. Each child could also have one sturdy storage box where they keep their bulkier treasures, one box per child. Encourage them to personalize their treasure box with pens, crayons, and pencils, and then use it to store their valuables. This helps confine messes that would otherwise spill out into their bedrooms or other areas of the house.

Keep what is important in a binder or treasure box. Enjoy your children's journals for many years to come. Once you have your tools and a system set up, it takes only minutes to find the right child's binder, punch paperwork, and put it behind the right year's divider.

THINK WITH YOUR BRAIN; REMEMBER WITH YOUR HAND

An organized person learns quickly that recording any important information, especially commitments with dates, times, and places, helps free the mind to think and decide, while keeping information safely stored on paper or the phone. Please don't use your brain for remembering. It is good most of the time, but lousy when it really matters—the more stress you have in your life, the less reliable is your remembering mind.

So as you practice being organized, make more complete notes by always writing down these three things:

1. The date something was said
2. Who said it
3. What was said

This allows you to go back to your notes and give them context. For example, a sticky note would indicate: "06.08.2018: Susan, neighbor party, July 10, 6:00 p.m., Greenery Park, bring main dish."

06.08.18: Susan, neighborhood party, July 10, 6:00 p.m., Greenery Park, bring main dish

Learn to make complete notes whenever you make any notes at all. Then practice getting this information to your permanent calendar (either your planner, computer, or phone). With this minimal information safely recorded, you can make additional notes to help with preparations. For example, on your calendar, note about one week before the party (on the day you regularly grocery shop) that you need to purchase hot dogs and buns for twelve. On your calendar several weeks before the party, note that you should mention this activity to your husband and children in your regular family council. (The concept of family councils will be addressed in more detail in chapter 9.)

USE PERMANENT LISTS

With your filing systems in place and having practiced the skill of making more complete notes when writing anything down, you are ready to take advantage of permanent lists. There are many reasons to keep permanent lists. Any time you do an activity once, you are more likely to do it again. So why not keep written records the first time, prepare a Permanent List form, keep these forms in your desktop filing system, and then add appropriate detailed notes each time you repeat the activity? An example is preparing and using master grocery lists. (The master grocery list concept will be explained further in chapter 7.) Soon you will have the patterns of success down pat. Whenever an activity repeats itself, you return to your permanent list, review it, edit it, and go forward with confidence.

You may choose to have personalized permanent to-do lists for "Picnics," "Trips," "Gifts Given," and "Guests." You can add permanent lists for major holiday preparations and keep them under the appropriate months' folders. For example, if you are preparing permanent lists for holidays, there could be several lists prepared for each holiday. Depending on the holidays you celebrate, these lists might be titled as follows:

- Holiday Meal
- Holiday Traditions
- Holiday Decorations
- Holiday Shopping
- Holiday Preparations (before holiday)
- Holiday Preparations (day of holiday)
- Holiday Cleanup (day after holiday)

If you plan to celebrate Thanksgiving at your home, your permanent holiday lists might be personalized as follows:

- Thanksgiving Meal
- Thanksgiving Traditions
- Thanksgiving Decorations
- Thanksgiving Shopping
- Thanksgiving Preparations (before Turkey Day)
- Thanksgiving Preparations (on Turkey Day)
- Thanksgiving Cleanup (after Turkey Day)

On each of the lists, indicate items specific to that list.

On the **Thanksgiving Meal** card, list the menu items you usually prepare for the Thanksgiving meal. Then, on the **Thanksgiving Shopping** list, indicate all the specialty items that you don't regularly have in your pantry or cupboards.

On the **Thanksgiving Traditions** list, indicate the special events you include on Thanksgiving, such as watching football games and giving to the food bank. This will remind you to rearrange furniture so company can watch football and to set aside canned goods to contribute to the local food bank.

On the **Thanksgiving Decorations** list, indicate where the Thanksgiving decorations are stored, where the turkey platter is hidden, and where Thanksgiving table napkins are tucked (and any items you don't want to have to try to remember from year to year).

On the **Thanksgiving Preparations (before Turkey Day)** list, indicate the chores you need to do to prepare for Thanksgiving Day (such as getting out the frozen turkey to thaw in the refrigerator, making and freezing rolls, making your pies so they can season in the refrigerator, and finding your bottled bread-and-butter pickles).

On the **Thanksgiving Preparations (on Turkey Day)** list, indicate the activities that will be important when you first get up, those that must be done after lunch, and, finally, those items you need to finish before you serve the big holiday meal.

Prepare these lists and refer to them year after year—occasionally adding to them as you learn how to be a better host or hostess. You can then prepare for holidays with confidence and reduce the hassle, frustration, and worry of any holiday season. Try it yourself and you will soon have your own collection of permanent lists for Thanksgiving, Christmas, New Year's Eve, New Year's Day, and every other holiday or recurring occasion for which you are personally responsible.

DO WHAT'S IMPORTANT
BEFORE IT BECOMES URGENT

As you become proficient at handling the flow of paperwork, you are ready to incorporate four time-management concepts that will change your life. I've taught these concepts in some of my other books because they are classic tools for time saving. Implement them consistently and you will see a major difference in the use of your time and you will begin to do what is important before it becomes urgent. Begin today to formally Plan, Prepare, Do, and Review!

Plan. Each day for the rest of your life, plan out your day. (Yes, you can relax a bit during vacations, but only if you aren't in charge of seeing that things go smoothly.) Walk through the day mentally, writing down the most important items that need your attention. First, note time commitments around which you will also complete your daily chores, errands, and cooking. For example, you carpool in the morning, so you will get gas and groceries afterward. Then you will unload the groceries and clean the kitchen before lunch.

Decide early in the day what you will serve for dinner. For most, it is not in the cooking that you will find the stress, but in the deciding. Decide and move forward planning for the day's other needs.

Make written note of items needing your attention (the odds and ends) that you will attempt to get to today if you have time around your firm commitments, housecleaning schedule, and the flexibility you need to meet the needs of the children, teenagers, and adults in your life. Write out this detailed plan before you begin the day.

Prepare. Once you have planned out your day on paper or computer, work through what you can do to prepare for the day. Do you need to get chicken parts out of the freezer for dinner? Do you need to put the two suits in the car to take to the dry cleaner? Do you need to call a neighbor to coordinate rides to the neighborhood birthday party this afternoon? Work through how you can prepare for the day to go more smoothly and you will be glad you did.

Do. As you go through your day, always ask yourself, "What is the best use of my time right now?" Try to work fast and remain focused on the day's home-management chores. Keep interruptions from outside sources—such as phone, media, and visitors—to a minimum until your housecleaning is done. Focus on your children when they need attention and work with them (as much as you can) to get their chores done properly. Finally, try to keep a balance between getting everything done and dealing with surprises. Sometimes you will meet a good friend unexpectedly, and by taking the time to visit for a few minutes, you will get thrown off your schedule. Still, a renewed friendship is worth the adjustment to your plans.

KEY CONCEPT: Tackle a fixing, mending, and replacing project. Fix one thing every day if you are primarily at home or one thing each weekend if you work full-time outside the home. Alter that pair of too-long pants, clean out the clogged bathroom drain, and replace the drill that won't turn on—no matter how much loving care it was given by your spouse.

Remember, tackle fix-it items regularly. Or write an invitation to your spouse about a mutually interesting weekend fix-it project and stick it on the refrigerator so he or she will know what this weekend might bring. With the whole family working on fixing, functional pacing will improve considerably.

Many benefits will come from regular, consistent focus on dedicated "doing." Your world will become more ordered and you will feel better about yourself for managing life's little challenges before they grow too big.

Review. At the end of the day, mentally walk back through the day and learn. What did you forget, neglect, or otherwise goof up? How can you avoid that ever happening again? Learn from the day's mistakes so tomorrow can be a better day. As an example, you might realize that immediately after exercising, you would do well to get a shower and dress for the day to save embarrassment when the doorbell rings. As you review each day, you will see changes and improvements that could be made. Then you can implement them the next day.

Plan, prepare, do, and review, and you will see significant improvements almost every single day in handling items of importance before they become urgent!

» 6 «

SIMULTANEOUS TO SEQUENTIAL WHEN STRESSED

Gain expertise in handling the inevitable stresses of life.

- *Action project:* Purge and organize the entry, living room, and family room
- Handle stressful seasons like a pro
- Manage grief and loss
- Welcome a new child

When stress increases, your ability to deal with different options, projects, and responsibilities diminishes. This is not because you are weak, bad, or otherwise faulty. It is just a fact of life! In this chapter, you will first learn how to create a veneer of order during the more difficult times of your life. You will do this by purging and organizing the entry, living room, and family room to present a welcoming, ordered area for those who come to the door or for a short visit. Then specific skills will be discussed about functioning well during stresses like bereavement, other losses, and transitions such as welcoming a new baby into the home.

PURGE AND ORGANIZE THE ENTRY, LIVING ROOM, AND FAMILY ROOM

The entry and living room are public statements of your lifestyle. Keep these areas free from most household items and strive to display your simple, stylish self.

Since people also live in your home, look at what seems to "live" in the entry and living room. Then make plans for improvement. Does the front coat closet need to be cleared of unused items so that something usually left on the entry floor can find a convenient home behind doors? Does the shoe basket need to be updated to accommodate the growing number of people in your home? Does it need to be relocated in the entry closet? Do your children and teenagers need training so their personal items don't land in the entry when they get home from school and extracurricular activities?

After making your assessment, go to work. Clean out, clean up, and make the entry and living room elegantly ordered and a reflection of your personal style. The entry benefits greatly from a bit of light and greenery. Where can you add a spot of light to make it more inviting? What bit of silk greenery will make the entry look homey and comfortable?

The living room also benefits from stylist comfort and a bit of formality. What can you change that will increase order and simplicity? Does the piano music need a better container? Does the number of pillows need to be reduced?

Most people who come to your front door won't go much beyond these areas—why not leave them impressed by organizing the entry and living room to make these areas more inviting? Why not feel confident when the front doorbell rings?

In some homes, the family room can be seen from the entry, so it is included here as a room that also needs purging. For the purposes of this book, the family room is less for formal company and more for casual use and the welcoming of good friends and family. It can usually be a little less neat and look a bit more lived in. Still, as you assess your family room, look for what can be purged to make it easier to keep it in a state of orderliness.

Do you need to put away a couple of the blankets that are usually kept on the couch—maybe in the closed, lower doors of a bookcase or tucked in the bottom of the end table? Does there need to be a wastebasket hidden somewhere close for discarding soda cans and gum wrappers? Do you need to buy a bigger container for the children's toys?

This room benefits from elements of warmth and comfort, and people need to be able to put their feet up, sit on the carpet, and set food and drinks down with ease and confidence. What does your family room need to make it both more orderly and appealing? Get to work cleaning out and cleaning up until you feel satisfied that this room meets your standards.

HANDLE STRESSFUL SEASONS LIKE A PRO

Now that you can feel comfortable about answering the front door even during seasons of stress, let's look at how to manage stress. Some seasons of life can be frustrating because schedules are messed up, contrary weather begins to wear you down, and the need for stability and sanity becomes paramount. Other times, the weeks may be extra heavy in the stress department because you keep having weeks like the last one. It catches up with you. You begin to feel overwhelmed. Add in unexpected company, a late night, and a few mishaps along the way, and disorganization is inevitable. Things can go bad—and seem to stay that way until stress becomes a daily partner. This reaction is normal and can happen many times during different seasons of life.

Coping skills will help you handle life when you are in a stressful situation or unfamiliar circumstances where things are not making much sense. Organize yourself to do what matters most first. This means that you move from more simultaneous living (doing a lot of things all at once) to somewhat sequential living (focusing on one priority, then another, and finally a third priority).

Become More Linear. When the going gets rough, tough, and otherwise impossible (even when it doesn't seem it should be that way from anyone else's point of view), it is time to become more linear and less spatial in your thinking and actions.

For instance, you awaken one morning and know it needs to be a "sequential" day. You are up late, you are not your best self, the housework seems endless, the children are out of sorts, and your mind is a fog about whether to start the dishes, get a batch of wash going, or just give up altogether and climb back in bed.

You know enough to avoid too many peripheral commitments during stressful times, because you are probably full to the brim with current responsibilities. You also know not to skimp on personal needs, personal primping, and personal renewal. But how do you manage overall?

Step Backward. The first step to bringing order back to your mind is to step back a pace or two. Look for an opportunity for nearly complete isolation, almost total quiet, and plenty of space. When you feel the need to get a grip, head toward your master bedroom if you are at home, go to the restroom if you are at work, or just take a walk (in either situation) so you can get away from the "noise." You need space to withdraw enough to see the trees within your forest. Sometimes the trees get too big and there are too many to see—so withdrawing allows you to better deal with the whole jungle.

Regroup. Regrouping includes reviewing your priorities, deciding if it is going to be cornflakes for dinner again, if the wash can be handled by your spouse, if your teenager can manage your two other children so you can have an hour alone at the library to work uninterrupted. In other words, review the options to do things differently—and maybe this time you'll do something that works better.

Unload on paper. List everything on your mind. Get it out on paper. Yes, everything. Then note whether these tasks are: "A" ("Must do today"), "B" ("Would like to get to this week"), "C" ("Can wait for later"), or "D" ("Aren't solvable, but still hurt"). (This procedure differs from that described in chapter 4 and chapter 12. In chapter 4, you learned how to use a to-do list to prepare before. Now, you can use this to-do list concept to reduce your immediate, pressing responsibilities, relieve stress, and proceed with more lineal living. In chapter 12, you will learn how to manage and resolve emotional needs using a different kind of list.)

Redo the lists. Divide your list into three different lists on separate sheets of paper. Put the "C" list in the back of your list stack. (It will be the last list to tackle.) Put the "B" list behind the first. (It will be there when and if you have energy to think about it.)

Face the highest priorities. Now take the "A" list. Number each item in your list and then decide the exact order in which you will face your day.

Yes, this technique takes a bit of time, but it will save trouble, decision-making, and lots of frustration for the rest of the day. With an ordered list of what to do, you now have focus. You can live SEQUENTIALLY. This will make it easier and faster to get going and keep going through the day. It will also get done what needs to be done most!

Go to work. Face the first item on your "A" list, tackle it, take care of it, and then go on to the next (between changing diapers, wiping noses, and answering questions if you have small ones in the home). Then go on to the second item (and answer phones, keep your boss happy, and smile at the customers if you are at work). Then move on to the third, fourth, and so on. You will get through the day and the rest of the week more successfully and happier than any other way.

Finish one smaller list item per day. As your confidence and capacity grows in managing your life sequentially, try every day to do one small additional thing that has been bothering you, doesn't take a lot of mental energy, and will stay done for awhile. These items usually aren't very important in and of themselves, but a feeling of increased control tends to return with any sort of permanent progress.

For instance, you might wipe off the sticky refrigerator shelf where you keep the milk. Or you might organize the gloves in the box at the top of the coat closet near the front door while waiting for the kids to come home from school. Or eliminate the cobwebs on the ceiling of your bedroom. Or go through your lipsticks and discard every single one that doesn't look good on you. Or go through the desk pens, find those that don't write, and discard them.

Try to do one thing every day to give yourself a sense of accomplishment. Choose several small, short, not-very-necessary things that have been bothering you—items to complete, to cross off, and to make you feel in control. Accomplishing something, anything, will make you feel in control when overwhelmed after stepping in the sticky milk and cold cereal that was spilled on the floor, when you are bothered by your baby's dirty diaper, or when you know there is another batch of laundry to fold. So choose several small, short, not-very-necessary things that have been bothering you, finish them, cross them off, and revel in your improved sense of control.

Whenever life becomes overwhelming and confusing in this way, the organized person works to slow down, recalibrate, and simplify. In other words, instead of living simultaneously and continuing to manage multiple projects and activities at once, there is movement to spend more time prioritizing and living sequentially. Use these concepts of linear living—all with the goal of being more ready for life's challenges.

Let's look now at principles for slowing down and managing life while dealing with high-stress situations such as bereavement and adding a new baby to the family.

MANAGE GRIEF AND LOSS

Sometimes life offers more stress than can be managed successfully, even by dedicated organization. This particularly happens during times of bereavement, trauma, or disaster. You are left bereft and struggle to face this new loss and keep up with your schedule. When this happens, it is all right to let it go. You are in mourning.

Let the business of your life go for awhile (without doing much explaining as to why you need a break), let the routines slide (without feeling guilty), and let your heart and mind soak in the new emotions and find a way to embrace these emotions (without trying to keep up with the rush of your obligations).

Move from simultaneous to more sequential living. You hurt, and the pain is real. You are in charge of letting it go until you can find new answers, more energy, and the healing of hope. When you hurt, remember that you don't always need to understand why you hurt; you just need to let life's pressures go while you make sense of your heart again.

Keep yourself together. Even while you mourn, however, you must keep up with five personal daily essentials:

- **Prayer**
- **Journaling**
- **Exercising**
- **Good grooming**
- **Dressing up**

Managing difficult emotions is easier when you seek spiritual connection, process your emotions by writing what you are feeling, get a bit of fresh air in your lungs, put a comb through your hair, and dress one level above your current mood. (Accessories always help.) These habits are essential even in the midst of despairing days.

Keep your personal environment together. When you are bereft, it helps to keep your home and family life together by focusing on five priorities:

1. **Meals**. Arrange for one good, hot meal for your family every day. They can fix the rest of the meals for themselves if they are old enough or you can scrounge from what you have if younger children need supervision.
2. **Laundry.** Keep up with the laundry either by having others do it or by putting one load in every day and getting it washed, dried, and put away.
3. **Paperwork.** Don't let the paperwork pile up. When the mail comes in, throw out all the junk. Open and pay as many of the bills as need immediate attention. Safely put aside paperwork that can be tackled later in your TO-DO, PENDING, BILLS, and TO FILE files. Or ask a trusted person to handle these needs for you.
4. **Entry and Front Room.** Keep the entry, living room, and family room neat (don't worry too much about keeping it clean) so that when company comes, you can answer the door and even visit a moment without embarrassment. Don't fuss with neatening the rest of the house unless you have family or friends willing to do it for you.

5. **Bathroom**. Finally, keep one or more bathrooms fresh and neat, both for company and for your own sanity.

Activate voluntary hibernation. Bereavement often brings too many people needing too much of your time and attention at a pace that is exhausting. Purposefully take as much time as needed to pull yourself away from other responsibilities and hibernate. Even though you may be at home, tell your family you are not "available" for a while. Go inside your favorite retreat and shut the door for some hibernation time. Turn off all "media" and just be with yourself. Feel. Think. Plan. Contemplate. Analyze. Settle down your heart. This multi-daily activity can help fill your emotional well and you can more easily move back to being with others.

Aloneness can help you think through to the end of your thoughts without interruption. It allows you to review and reflect. You can come out of hibernation an easier-to-live-with person, more capable of coping and healing. You can move closer to a state of equilibrium and energy.

It is up to you to say no, maybe not at that moment, and maybe just a little bit later. It is up to you to look at your problems and always move toward solutions that function better for you and yours. Move from feeling like madness is descending into your life to a place of being more settled. You will feel better, you'll see things with greater clarity, and you'll be better able to endure the sometimes long, wearying days.

WELCOME A NEW CHILD

Another season of significant stress that requires movement from simultaneous to sequential living is the arrival of a new child in the home. Apply specific skills for this adjustment and relieve the stress level of the whole family.

The new normal. After the birth of a baby, most families want to return to "normal" as soon as possible, not realizing that their new situation means that their "old" normal will never be possible because there has been a sweet addition to their home. This principle is also useful to anyone going through a transition in life, such as children leaving for the military, college, or marriage. There is no returning to the "old" normal; there is only looking toward the "new" normal. So instead of trying to return to the "old" normal, you must determine what a "new" normal will look like.

Limit outside commitments. Caring for a baby and giving him or her the attention needed, plus taking care of your own health, the house, and the rest of the family, can be overwhelmingly exhausting. For at least three months (or about when the baby is sleeping through the night and the parents' fatigue level is going down), don't take on anything more and limit energy spent on previous commitments. Consider this phrase: "I will give no more than 50 percent to anything outside my immediate family circle."

Say "No, thank you." Learn the beauty of the word "NO," because every time you say *no* to anything and everything outside the absolute necessities, you are saying *yes* to precious time with the new baby, other family members (who are also getting used to the "new" normal), and yourself. This is precious time to center your energies inward.

Say "Yes, please." Learn to say "YES," because every time you let someone else help you, you will reap the benefits of increased peace and capacity. Let others do your normal housekeeping, fold your wash, run your errands, and bring in meals. Say "YES" whenever they offer. Be specific about how you might be helped: "Yes, I could use some milk. Could you buy two gallons and also pick up a bunch of bananas for me?" Or "Yes, I do have some mending that needs attending to. Can I leave it on my front porch, as I'm just off to take a nap while the baby sleeps and the kids are at school?" Or "Yes, I would love to have you fix dinner for me tonight. Thanks for knowing that two weeks into raising a baby is the perfect time for an evening without fixing a meal."

When you begin to return to regular housework, ignore any major cleaning, scrubbing, or organizing. Mostly focus on "neatening." (More on these concepts can be found in chapter 3.) Remember that neatening up your home makes it look 80 percent clean. The rest of the housecleaning needs can probably wait until your energy returns, the baby begins to sleep through the night, and regular routines can be restored. Like in other seasons of stress, focus on five priorities:

- **Meals.** Arrange for one hot family meal per day.
- **Laundry.** Keep the washer and dryer humming. Laundry needs increase with the addition of a new baby to the home.

- **Paperwork.** Discard junk mail, pay the bills, and safely file other paperwork to address later.
- **Entry and front room.** Keep these areas neat and inviting for unexpected company.
- **Bathroom.** Keep the most-used bathroom neat and clean.

Go slow. Finally, be kind to yourself and go slow. If you don't feel like company yet, ask for a rain check when people suggest they stop by. If you don't feel like going out yet, suggest a later date. If you don't feel like taking on too much housework, then rest. Soon enough, your energy and capacity will return. In the meantime, give that baby a kiss and remember to say to yourself: "Fifty percent. I'll just give 50 percent until I feel ready to fully embrace this 'new' normal in my life."

— » 7 « —

FAST FOOD
TO FINE FOOD

Never have to decide what to serve for dinner again.

- **Action project:** Purge and organize the kitchen
- Take the decisions out of menu planning
- Employ superior grocery-shopping skills
- Improve cooking skills

Setting up a functional kitchen is essential to better home management. Then you can conquer food management, meal preparation, and food-storage skills to add significant extra time to each day—plus reduce personal stress. It takes a bit of extra work to set up a Master Menu and a Master Grocery List and to keep written records of best prices, but the freedom of knowing what you will cook for every meal, except for those times of celebration or pleasure, makes for a happy, peaceful home.

PURGE AND ORGANIZE THE KITCHEN

Next to the bathrooms, the kitchen is probably the most active place in the home and is often in a state of flux. After all, you eat there several times a day, gather there for conversations and fun, and walk through it many times on your way to and from other activities.

Getting the kitchen organized improves personal and family organization. How can you help your kitchen help you? Start with six main projects:

- **Increase counter space**
- **Empty out cupboards**
- **Organize the cupboards**
- **Put tools at the point of first use**
- **Expedite table setting and cleanup**
- **Organize the refrigerator and pantry**

Increase counter space. The practical advantage of having counters cleared as much as possible is simple: if there isn't clutter on the counters, they are easier to clean. With emptier counters, the kitchen seems to expand. There is more space for cooking, baking, and other projects. Most kitchen counters are "decorated" with small appliances, trinkets, a spouse's knickknacks, children's schoolwork, and an assortment of other treasures. It is time to decide which items can be cleared off permanently.

Ask yourself this question: "Is the item a friend or freeloader?" Friends are kitchen tools that are frequently used or too oversized or too heavy to go elsewhere (like a microwave). Such tools as a KitchenAid or another mixer (if it is used frequently) are rightful placeholders on the counter, especially if you have an L-shaped kitchen and a large counter corner. Other tools can be stored in the cupboard or on a shelf. Paper towels, for example, are useful tools that can be hung under the upper cabinets, thus eliminating a lifetime of lifting and cleaning the holder each time the counters are wiped down.

Freeloaders, which are infrequently used tools or trinkets, should be stored elsewhere or even sent to charity, because the trouble of maintaining them outweighs their usefulness in the kitchen.

So remove all the items from your kitchen counters and then ask a simple question before returning any item: Is this a friend or a freeloader?

Because kitchens are primarily for working, add décor to the walls to make the kitchen inviting and still make it easy to keep neat and clean. How much nicer it is to have clearer counters! You will notice how much easier it is to work in your kitchen and how much time you save.

Empty out cupboards. Kitchen cupboards are meant to be helpful, so let's help the kitchen cupboards help you—it is time to think "purge" again.

Generally, cleaning out the cupboards means removing all the items, wiping down the shelves, and then making decisions.

As you begin to systematically purge, consider reducing the tools that you rarely use and increasing the tools that you use more frequently. For example, a stove usually has only four elements, so as was also explained in chapter 2, having an overabundance of pans in "A" storage areas around the stove doesn't use that space well. Store your favorite four pans, unstacked, in an "A" place and store the other pans in "B" or "C" kitchen or pantry areas. You will find cooking much easier, with far less hassle.

On the other hand, having multiple measuring spoons and cups makes organizational sense, especially if you are always looking for them in the dishwasher. You may want to keep up to three sets on hand. This will facilitate having one ready to use at all times (one clean, one in use, and one in the dishwasher).

There might be kitchen items that you are not sure whether to keep, share, or toss. Take these "I'm not sure about" items and put them in temporary storage in another part of your house. Retrieve the tools as needed during the next week or so. Leftovers still in the box after that time can be stored in "B" or "C" areas or given away.

Organize the cupboards. Items that are used frequently should be stored in "A" places, such as the top row of drawers, the lower shelf of your upper cupboards, and the front areas of your lower cupboards.

Keep only "A" tools in the top drawers. Most kitchens only need three knives in an "A" drawer: a large, a small, and a serrated knife. Store other "A" tools in these drawers, too, but store needed but used-less-frequently tools somewhere else.

Items that are used less often go in "B" places. These are drawers and shelves where you have to stretch up or bend over to reach the needed item. Rarely used tools can go in "C" places, the rear of shelves, lowest drawers, or highest cupboards.

Items that are used even less often go in "D" places, such as the shelving in kitchen corners.

In addition, "unstack unlikes." As an example, have separate stacks for large mixing bowls and smaller mixing bowls. On the other hand, "stack alikes." Items that are the same shape can be stacked (mixing bowls, plastic storage containers, or plastic drinking glasses).

Because the other hand usually is wet, dirty, or holding a child, strive to retrieve any kitchen tool with just one hand: one hand to get out a knife, one hand to bring down a bowl, one hand to retrieve a pan.

Kitchen cupboards are meant to keep kitchen tools convenient and orderly. Everything can go that clogs that process, gets in the way, or is just not needed. Cleaning out and organizing your kitchen cupboards will significantly contribute to your personal well-being and make cooking a time-saving project.

Put tools at the point of first use. In addition to storing items according to "A," "B," "C," or "D" spacing, consider storing kitchen items at the point of their first use. There are three main kitchen areas: the sink, the stove, and the mixing counter. Put appropriate tools near where they will be used for the chores of these three centers. For example, peelers belong close to the kitchen sink. Dish soap, scrubbers, and dish racks should be right there too. Spices should be close to the stove. The stove is also where you stir foods, scramble them, and flip them over. Spatulas, stirring spoons, and wooden tools should be stored nearby. Pans and their lids should be in the immediate vicinity. The cupboards near the mixing counter should hold measuring spoons and cups, baking spices, and mixing bowls to make mixing quick and easy.

The best way to see if your kitchen has tools stored at their "place of best use" is to stand at each of the work centers and reach for your commonly used tools. Can you stand in one place and reach the pans? Can you get the peeler without moving from the sink? Can you mix a cake without moving around a lot? Every time a tool is moved nearer to its place of first use, you will save seconds here and there each time you are in the kitchen.

Expedite table setting and cleanup. Setting the table is often a laborious task. One way to simplify this daily chore is to take all needed items from the cupboards and drawers when it is time to set the table. Put these items in a large plastic bin, carry the bin to the table, and go to work. Wow, just one trip from the kitchen to the table does the job! Use the same bin to gather dirty dishes after the meal and you will find that, again, it only takes one trip. Of course, this method would not work for your fancy china!

Organize the refrigerator and pantry. Using these same principles, organize the refrigerator and pantry to be more useful to family members. Both these areas are high-maintenance creatures. If you neglect their maintenance, it will come back to haunt you every time you open their doors. So set up a maintenance schedule and stick to it. Many home managers find that a quick pantry "spiff up" before grocery shopping each week works well, along with an equally quick "wipe down" of the refrigerator shelves. You not only see what needs replenishing, but you can also organize these areas again.

Finally, as you purge and organize your kitchen, remember that you will be making a mess. Out goes the obsolete, aged, and broken— all with the goal to get rid of half. Useful but unneeded items can be donated. Useful and needed items can be stored at the point of first use. Your organized refrigerator and pantry can also serve you better. All in all, your kitchen will be dramatically improved.

TAKE THE DECISIONS OUT OF MENU PLANNING

After the kitchen and pantry are in order, the next step is to move from "fast food to fine food" by putting together a Master Menu. Make a simple, one-page plan listing seven options for breakfast and lunch. This part of the Master Menu can be rotated on a weekly basis. Then list a variety of main meals you will serve on a monthly rotating basis. A young mother with picky eaters may find that setting up seven evening meals on a rotating basis keeps the kids happy and the cook even happier. Two people might find that a two-week dinner Master Menu suits their needs because they cook one night and eat leftovers the next. More exotic cooks might find they want to have one month's worth of different meals before they duplicate menus again. The concept is to set something up and then rotate through the Master Menus without having to make any decisions.

The Master Menu format. If, for example, a home manager is comfortable with a four-week outline, his or her Master Menu form would include columns for "Day of the week," "bread," "vegetable," and "fruit." It is most useful not only to list the days of the week, but also to give each day an official name to categorize the meals:

- **Monday**—Easy
- **Tuesday**—Mexican
- **Wednesday**—Poultry
- **Thursday**—Beef
- **Friday**—Italian
- **Saturday**—Fast Meals
- **Sunday**—Breakfast for Dinner

After listing seven menu categories for seven days, list four favorite meals for each of these days. For example, under "Tuesday—Mexican" would be listed four different Mexican meals, as seen below:

- **Monday**
- **Tuesday**—Mexican
    - » Soft tacos
    - » Hard tacos
    - » Enchiladas
    - » Taco salad
- **Wednesday**
- **Thursday**
- **Friday**
- **Saturday**
- **Sunday**

The Master Menu details. Next, list a bread (if you need to fill teenage or adult stomachs), a vegetable, and a fruit appropriate for that day's main meal. These three items are served repeatedly each week, although the main dish varies for each day. For instance, using the four-week Master Menu, every Tuesday you might serve corn muffins, corn (frozen or canned), and mandarin oranges—but the main meals will rotate through soft tacos, hard tacos, enchiladas, and taco salad.

Repeat the process. Use this same process for each day of the week, listing four main meals, a bread, a vegetable, and a fruit. You will then have twenty-eight meals, seven breads, seven vegetables, and seven fruits listed. This Master Menu serves as the basis for your weekly meal planning, your grocery shopping, and your cooking routine. You will find your family settling into a schedule as they anticipate Italian food on Fridays and breakfast for dinner on Sundays. You will have a system to prepare meals in a timely manner and will always know what to say when someone asks, "What are we having for dinner tonight?"

Make up recipe cards. Once you have decided on your menus, it is useful to make up 3" x 5" recipe cards for each main meal and keep them in a 3" x 5" recipe box behind seven card dividers. Label these blank card dividers "Sunday," "Monday," "Tuesday," "Wednesday," "Thursday," "Friday," and "Saturday." The Master Menu recipes are stored behind the Master Menu (Sunday through Saturday) dividers in the front of the recipe box.

Organizing sufficiently, including knowing exactly where the recipes are for each meal, makes the process for preparing meals simpler and faster on every level.

As a side note, your other printed recipes can be kept behind these easy-to-retrieve recipes using traditional recipe card dividers, which are often listed by topic. Use this second set of card dividers for all viable but less-frequently-used recipes.

Keep only the very best recipes. It takes only one good brownie recipe to keep a family happy.

EMPLOY SUPERIOR GROCERY-SHOPPING SKILLS

Shopping is an "expensive" time consumer. You have to travel, park, walk through the store, make decisions, wait to be checked out, and then travel again. Sometimes you are also coping with children, managing a work schedule, and fitting this trip to the store around other priorities. Going shopping for necessities just isn't that fun for the busy home manager. One of the best ways to save time is to make grocery shopping more efficient. For most, the following practices make a significant dent in the amount of time spent shopping.

- Prepare a **Master Grocery List** that indicates all the foods you will need to fix the meals on your Master Menu. You may find it easiest to lay out this Master Grocery List by topic, or you may find it easier to list the foods in order of how you shop at your favorite grocery store.

- **Make fifty-two copies.** Make enough copies for one year's use and store the spare forms in your desktop filing system. (See chapter 5 for effectively using your desktop filing system.)

- **Post the Master Grocery List.** Keep the Master Grocery List on your refrigerator for easy noting of items that need replacing. After inventorying your pantry, cupboards, refrigerator, and freezer, review the grocery ads and use the Master Grocery List to also note which items you will obtain at discount.

- **Shop with your tools.** Shop with your printed Master Grocery List on a clipboard that has a calculator on the clip to facilitate price comparison.

- **Track best prices.** Track prices for frequent purchases with a system that works for you. You might like to keep written records, use your phone, or keep an updated list on an Excel worksheet. When you know what a good price is, you can make purchases with confidence.

- **Buy cheap.** Take advantage of sales, discounts, and closeouts using internet comparison shopping and local printed ads.

- **Watch for lowest prices.** Note possible "future" purchases as you shop, but don't buy yet. In other words, hold off what you want but don't yet need until you get the best price. Then purchase in bulk.
- **Need one, buy two.** Buy by doubles, by triples, or by the year to save time, trouble, and transportation costs. For example, if you need a bag of shredded coconut, buy two bags. If you need salad dressing, buy two bottles. If you are getting a bottle of catsup, buy two. So do yourself a favor and never go to the store without thinking, *If I need one, I'll buy two!*
- **Buy by the year.** Of course, this is only the first level of saving time when you shop. Conscientious home managers trying not just to save "some" time but to double and triple time savings will go one step further. They will need one and buy three or four or even enough for the whole year. The goal is simple: Don't go to the store for anything without coming home with two, three, or four things! Your life will be simplified, your time will expand, and as much as you might love to be out shopping, save that time for the fun kind!
- **Use a date stamp.** Date stamp items and store your purchases in convenient storage areas. Stock your home with as many of your grocery store items as possible! (See chapter 11 for skills for putting away nonfood items by the year.)

IMPROVE COOKING SKILLS

Because eating out consumes a great deal of time, an organized person might want to increase home cooking skills to make getting meals on the table a simple project. Improving several cooking skills will aid in this goal.

- **Cook in bulk.** Always cook enough food for at least two meals and freeze the leftovers for the next week's meal or to use later this week.
- **Cook meat for four meals.** Always cook enough meat for four meals. For example, use one half of the cooked chicken for the meal at hand and the anticipated leftover meal. Take the other

half of the cooked chicken and freeze it for two future meals. If you serve chicken four times in a month, then in one cooking session you can cook enough for the whole month.

- **Cook perfect pasta.** Learn to cook pasta the perfect way. Fill the pasta pot with water to the normal level. Add salt and oil as you are wont to do. Bring the water to a heavy boil. Add the pasta, stir thoroughly, and turn off the source of heat. Cook the pasta without further disturbance for one and one-half times the usual suggested cooking time. You will have perfect pasta every time without cloudy water, broken pieces, and overcooked noodles. Add cooked meat, red or white sauce, and grated cheese for a quick meal.

- **Cook better rice.** Learn to cook white and brown rice so that it is tender and delicious. A rice cooker is the best method, but using microwave recipes can also be successful. Remember that as rice ages it needs more moisture to cook properly. Add cooked meat, a bit of sauce, and vegetables for an expedient dinner.

- **Bake a fluffy potato.** Learn to successfully bake potatoes in the microwave or oven. This will help you put together a potato bar with the addition of heated leftovers.

- **Serve nutritious meals.** Plan to serve five different items at each meal for complete nutrition. You can think of your five fingers when making this calculation. For example, a spaghetti meal with salad, oranges, and milk has the five elements of good nutrition: calcium (milk), starch (pasta), protein (meat), vegetables (pasta sauce and salad), and fruit (oranges). Teach your children how to calculate if the planned meal has complete nutrition; just hold up your hand and list the items.

- **Change up your Master Menu.** Once you get a recipe down and don't mind putting it together, add it to your Master Menu, add the necessary items to your Master Grocery List, and practice putting the recipe together with greater and greater efficiency.

Simple meals are just as efficient as trips to the local drive-through. The thoughtful home manager saves time by becoming a skilled shopper and cook.

—— » 8 « ——

FRIVOLOUS TO FOCUSED FINANCES

Work toward financial constancy, one step at a time.

- *Action project:* Organize acquisition routines
- Create a family spending creed
- Implement a family budget
- Rid yourself of all debt
- Employ five rules for fair fighting

If you want to have more time, stop spending money. Beyond grocery needs, your purchasing patterns are probably still taking a great deal of your time. This chapter focuses on skills that can save time and money for you and your family. These skills include changing up acquisition routines, developing a family spending creed to unify your family's financial goals and focus, implementing a family budget, ridding yourself of debt, and employing new skills when contention arises over finances. Let's look at each of these principles to see how to implement them. Let's also review the benefits from following them consistently.

ORGANIZE ACQUISITION ROUTINES

Because shopping takes a lot of time and energy, the organized person is always looking for ways to reduce the amount of time spent shopping, whether it is time spent in stores or online.

Reduce acquisition and accumulation patterns. Do you suffer from the bad habit of acquiring and then returning something? When you are shopping, do you feel more worthwhile? How much time and effort does it cost you to return items? If you care to reverse this trend in small ways and make long-lasting organizational improvements in your life, think about ways you can change your shopping at holidays, birthdays, and other significant celebrations.

Simplify gift giving. Inform everyone that you are going to go simple. For example, at Christmastime, you might indicate there will be one big gift and one small surprise per adult in your immediate family (past what Santa may bring), a simple group gift for those at work, a very small gift for friends and neighbors who come to the door to exchange holiday greetings, and a meaningful gift for that special someone in your life.

Gift shop differently. Give tools rather than trinkets. These are gifts that keep on giving every time they are picked up and used. For example, during the winter holidays, buy slippers for cold mornings at home, small LED flashlights for peers at work, and a box of wooden matches and a candle in a sealed clear glass jar for neighbors and nearby friends who can use them for "blackout" emergencies.

Decide what to give beforehand. Another way to save time is to decide once and for all what you will give when you are invited to bridal showers, baby showers, birthdays, and special occasions. For example, you might decide to give a four-way screwdriver at all bridal showers, sleeved bibs for baby showers, bills rolled inside of blown-up balloons at birthdays, and restaurant gift certificates for presents that need to be mailed. Always look for ways to stay away from the store. Decide what you will give and then buy in bulk. Pretty soon people will know what you give and may even look forward to getting your specialized gift.

Spending less time shopping is a good first step toward saving more time.

CREATE A FAMILY SPENDING CREED

Have a long-term, family-wide spending creed to save money, contention, and time.

Live on less than earned. The first spending creed goal is to live on less than you earn. So the goal next month is to spend less than that month's income. For instance, if your family nets $2,000 per month, then the goal is to spend less than $1,999 during that same month. The next goal is to put enough money into savings over the twelve months so you can use the previous month's money to pay the current month's bills. This habit means that you are living on less than you earn and that you are financially ahead by one month. This is the beginning of financial stability.

Consult together. Your money creed should also include how much each spouse can spend without consulting the other. For example, a young couple might set up the following standard while in school. Each will get $25 in cash per month to spend without having to explain to anyone how it was spent. Each of you may spend up to $10 from the family budget without consulting the other (except for grocery money, which is spent within the allowance you have agreed upon). Past those amounts, consult when a purchase is significant enough to be considered an "investment." For example, you may decide not to spend more than $100 on an item without coming away from the store, discussing the impact of the purchase in private, and agreeing upon where the money will come from to make the purchase.

You might also decide not to spend more than $500 without considerable research (meaning studying consumer reviews and product comparisons), seeking advice of others who have used the same product, and sleeping on a purchase decision. For example, it is prudent to research washing machines through consumer reviews, talk to repair personnel, and check with others' experiences before purchasing a new machine.

This pattern, while taking more time at the moment, saves both money and time over the long run.

Save money creatively. Part of a family spending creed can be to agree on creative ways to increase your current skills and learn new ones to save time and money. For example, learning how to cut children's hair makes trips to the barber obsolete and allows for parent-child interactions at the same time. Deciding to eat out once a month and on special occasions allows for celebrations away from the kitchen, but it also limits the amount of money spent on fast food. Time and money are saved with each decision you make about how to spend your money and with each skill that you conquer and don't depend on others for. This also offers more schedule flexibility and the fun of learning to live "thin."

In addition, you should take advantage of making money in the margins to help pad the available family money. Learning a skill such as tole painting or sewing custom children's clothing, teaching piano lessons, or editing term papers can all be done in the margins of your personal time to help with family finances.

IMPLEMENT A FAMILY BUDGET

The constrictiveness of a family budget and the time spent balancing it is offset by the security of knowing that you have the best possible method to meet your financial obligations and that all family members are on the same page. Short-term restraint that is self-imposed when sticking to a budget results in long-term discipline and financial benefits. It is not easy to spend less than you would like financially, but it is important to have common long-term goals. It is worth every older couch you recover, every article of clothing you wear past its prime, and every homemade meal you prepare!

Don't spend what you don't have. A significant improvement in spending habits happens when the family stops using credit cards. This can be done with "plastic surgery" (meaning cutting up all your cards but one, which can be saved for emergencies). For the reluctant spouse, it can be done differently. Put the cards in the bottom of a plastic carton, fill the carton with water, and put the carton in your freezer. The cards are available, but only with great effort.

The habit of paying cash for goods (using a debit card, checks, or actual money) will help you avoid a great many financial problems. Just because you want it doesn't mean that you have to get it. When the pain of payment and the pleasure of acquisition happen at the same time, responsible financial resourcing has begun.

Once you decide to be a saving expert, you can work to make every single dollar stretch as far as possible. This means learning to be frugal and conservative. It means learning to repaint instead of replace, mend instead of purchase, and find contentment with the current situation.

RID YOURSELF OF ALL DEBT

Financial distress can be a great burden in your life, whether it arises from consumer debt, vehicle debt, or a mortgage. It is not a lifestyle any of you would choose, but it is one you are often caught in. Sometimes the black hole of debt looms bigger and bigger in your life until it becomes so overwhelming you decide to just give up and hope things "will work out."

So the final big financial goal is to begin a determined plan to rid yourselves of all debt, including consumer debt, vehicle debt, and housing debt. (And, yes, some of you haven't even gotten your first car or purchased a home, but read on—your future may be better than you think.) While this is a big project, it is fulfilling and saves time down the line because a lack of indebtedness means that less time needs to be spent earning money, because costs are inevitably less as debts are paid off.

Debt doesn't have to be in your life forever. It doesn't have to rob you of precious pennies, valuable dollars, and a good night's sleep. It just doesn't. You can begin today to turn the corner, change your circumstances, and find answers. The process is easy to begin, and it is worth every sacrifice you will have to make.

Here are the steps to financial constancy:

1. **Stop using credit cards as the preferred method of payment.** In addition, forestall using credit cards for smaller emergencies by putting away a substantial bit of money for any potential emergencies in a new "Emergencies" savings account at your

local bank. Continue putting extra dollars into this account. When there is enough stashed for you to feel comfortable, you can confidently set aside your credit cards because you have money saved for emergencies. Then you are ready for a focused reduction of debt. (Continuing to use a debit card is all right because that is like paying cash.)

2. **Detail to whom you owe money**, usually listing from top to bottom the smallest debt to the largest debt.

3. **List how much you owe** to each of these creditors and the corresponding interest rates.

4. **List monthly payments** for consumer debt, vehicle loans, and home mortgages. Then calculate how much of each month's payment is going toward interest and how much is going toward principal reduction. This can be accomplished by using an amortization calculator on the internet or obtaining an amortization schedule from your financial institution. This information will help you realize how much you can save by getting out of debt.

5. **Begin with the smallest debt and work toward its demise**. While it may make more sense to pay off the debt with the highest interest rate, tick off the smallest debt to gain momentum and confidence at ridding yourself from debt. You might make up a visual reminder, using graph paper and drawing squares to represent the amount left to pay off. A labeled glass jar is also helpful for collecting cash you choose not to spend in favor of paying off this debt.

6. **Continue to pay regular monthly payments** on all other debts—even as you strive to eliminate this smallest debt. Plan to "snowball" this smallest debt's monthly payment toward your next smallest debt when this first debt is gone. In other words, continue to spend the same amount each month in debt servicing, but accelerate your progress toward eliminating debt.

7. **Focus your energies and keep on track.** Begin your trek to financial freedom. No matter your circumstances, no matter the amount of debt, you need to know the truth about your obligations and begin to pay them off!

EMPLOY FIVE RULES FOR FAIR FIGHTING

When finances are discussed, couples often find they move quickly from talking to fighting. Five rules will help you return to discussion mode successfully. They are applicable to financial discussions but also to other home and family challenges. Peace in your family life can be threatened when you and yours, at the most unexpected times, become emotionally escalated over any number of things.

Because it is likely that a couple of fights will blow up as soon as you settle into your financial constancy path, here are five rules to share with your spouse so the two of you can fight fairly. (This is just a fancy way of setting definitive boundaries so the noise will be contained, the Band-Aids will last a bit longer, and peace can be restored in a relatively short time.) If you work with your spouse to resolve conflicts in this way, you will be surprised how much better things will be.

- **Rule #1. Cool down first.** If you are really, really mad, you must have a cool-down period and isolate yourself from the problem. Then you can invite the other person to a "discussion" of the issues.
- **Rule #2. Try to see the other side.** Most "fights" are caused by the inability to clearly see another's point of view. Looking at the situation without being emotionally involved can help focus the discussion.
- **Rule #3. No hitting, either physically or verbally.** If you need to resolve a conflict, you must do it kindly with your mouth and not with your fists. Hitting hurts irreparably. Unkind words can hurt, too, so both are off-limits.
- **Rule #4. Talk nicely.** If you need to clash with words, do not use profanity, gutter language, or bathroom or bedroom words. There is no name calling or sassing. You must also use your "inside" voice. You must stay on topic, writing down other areas of conflict for discussion later.
- **Rule #5. Propose a solution to the problem at hand.** Conflict is normal, but you must work through it, find answers, and still keep the peace. Get past the conflict and on with the negotiations. What answer will work best this time?

As a spouse, these five rules can prove invaluable when discussing finances. Five rules, enough for each finger of one hand. Cool down, see the other side, don't hit, talk nicely, and propose a solution!

Use this skill set to help make discussing finances just a little bit easier. Work to resolve conflicts over finances and much of your familial stress will be reduced—and a great deal of time will be saved!

— » 9 « —

PANICKED
TO PACED

Life's surprises
will come,
but you can
be ready.

- *Action project:* Organize weekly family councils
- Simplify at all levels
- Make your day like a dance
- Start less; end earlier

In this chapter, you will focus on four pacing skills that, when practiced consistently, will help move your lifestyle from panicked to paced—with the result of saving time and energy. Let's start by organizing the family.

ORGANIZE WEEKLY FAMILY COUNCILS

A family is like a complex machine. There are comings and goings, commitments in different directions, rides that must be coordinated, and responsibilities that need to be delegated. A business wouldn't function well without a regular planning meeting. A family also benefits from careful weekly planning. When you begin to have weekly meetings with all family members living in the same space (whether that be two or twenty), you will find that coordination begins to flow and conflict starts to flee. Either you talk about the upcoming week and work through how to best make it happen, or you end up fighting about it when time is short and the pressure is on. Holding weekly family meetings takes time to save time! Let's get things set up using tools, systems, and routines.

The family council: Tools. A family calendar is an important tool for writing down items of importance in a place that all family members can see. After it is filled in during the weekly family council, which will be spoken about presently, it can be conveniently posted near the kitchen table, where it can be referred to every night to reiterate what the next day will bring.

A larger calendar is better because it allows more space for keeping details in one place. This calendar is for your whole family's use. Once it is purchased, label the calendar right away with known commitments, family birthdays, holiday plans, youth camps, and extended family reunion dates. Help all family members know that getting their personal priorities onto the family calendar is essential for a smooth-running family.

Colorful stickers can be added to emphasize important dates (for example, hearts for Valentine's Day and balloons for birthdays). Using small stickers for regular, repeating events helps remind the family of their commitments. In other words, blue stickers on Tuesdays are a reminder of piano lessons, green stickers on Wednesday remind family members about soccer practice, and pink stickers point out dance lessons are on Friday. Even the youngest members of the family can easily learn to associate the colored stickers with commitments in their lives.

Bright stickers with colors designated for each family member are also useful. If Tom's color is yellow, then a yellow sticker next to details about time and place act as a reminder that he is going to the dentist next Tuesday.

The family calendar should be located in a prominent place for easy viewing and to facilitate taking down and rehanging as items are added to the calendar. The family calendar should be updated as soon as commitments are known. For example, add the date, time, and place for a family wedding reception upon receipt of the invitation. Keep the invitation in the appropriate "1–31" desktop file folder about one week before the event, and then check to see if you have an appropriate gift to wrap. At the beginning of each month, review the calendar and add additional notes to help your days go better. If Kevin's birthday is on the fifteenth, when will you take him birthday shopping? Note that date on the calendar. If you have a traditional family party on the twenty-fifth, when will you go to the ethnic store and purchase the supplies for that special dessert you always bring? Also note this errand on the calendar.

As explained before, after you become aware of activities and commitments, it is time to add "launch" and "land" time periods to your calendar to minimize last-minute pressures and stress. Plan an hour for "launching" and an hour for "landing" around each major activity. This allows sufficient time for preparations and sufficient time to put things away after being out and about. Plan for a day of "launching" and a day of "landing" around each family trip or vacation. Also, plan about a week for "launching and landing" between major seasonal transitions such as the beginning and ending of school, winter holidays, and vacations.

Mark these time periods on your calendar as though they were appointments. Actually, they are appointments, but just with you and yours. This gives you permission to take time to pack for an upcoming trip and unload the refrigerator of items that will slime, smell, or self-destruct during your vacation. It allows you time to have a day to wash, answer emails, and pay the bills when you come home after a few days' absence.

KEY CONCEPT: In addition to these calendar preparations, help family members create a back-it-up schedule for bigger projects that need to be broken into smaller bites. This makes progress toward the bigger goal easier.

For example, preparing a **back-it-up calendar** for your ninth grader's major ten-page English paper, which is due in seven weeks, would include these activities:

1. Print a small personal calendar of the current and next month.
2. Note the due date of the English paper.
3. Plan to have the paper ready three days before it is due by going backward to allow three days for printing, mess-ups, and illness.
4. Back up to allow for three days for final editing and proofing.
5. Back up to allow three weeks for writing the ten pages.
6. Back up to allow two weeks for research and outlining.
7. Back up to allow one week to designate the topic.

Each week at the family meeting, the ninth grader can be invited to update the family on his paper progress and where he might need additional support. If every family member receives this type of attention and support, panicked preparations will give way to stabilizing pacing.

Once your calendar is prepared, quickly review what tomorrow will bring at the beginning of the evening meal. Remind family members of their commitments and responsibilities. For instance, "George, tomorrow I will be picking you up at school to take you to piano lessons." "Mary, you need to make cupcakes for that party tomorrow. After dinner, I will help you bake them." "Frank, when would be a good time to gas up for the drive to the wedding up north?" The family calendar can act as a prompter to help family activities run smoothly and lessen the stress that can often accompany a busy family's life.

The family council: Tools. At the beginning of the year, purchase a family calendar and notate all known events on it. Review and make detailed plans at the beginning of the month. Have a family council and coordinate activities at the beginning of the week and go over the calendar at dinner time.

The family council: Systems. Family councils are a three-part meeting. First, parents meet, then the family meets, and then the parents meet with each child individually. Let's see how this would work.

Part one of family council: Just the parents. First, the parents meet to coordinate the activities for the upcoming week, speak of the children's needs, and work through any outstanding intra- and inter-family conflicts or issues.

- **Coordinate activities** for the upcoming week and make notes on the family calendar: "You will be gone Tuesday evening, so I will babysit. I will be gone Thursday evening; can you take the children?" "How about we get a babysitter so we can attend the wedding reception on Friday?" "I will call the plumber to get the repair done. How about making arrangements to be home on Thursday during lunch to let him in?" The more you plan together and come to common consensus, the greater will be your confidence to go forward with your week and know that things are in place to happen as the family needs.

- **Address children's needs.** If you have children or others who live with you, speak of their needs: "John has been getting up too late to leave for school on time, and I have been driving him. What are we going to do to change that?" "Mary is hitting Paul when they play together. How will we address that issue?" "Sue is behind on her reading. What shall we do?" Problems are brought up and discussed, and plans are made for solutions. Then parents can work together to coordinate how they will proceed.

- **Working through outstanding issues**. For example, "My sister is still nagging me to take that scrapbooking class next month. What do you think? Can we handle the necessary arrangements for me to be gone once a week?" "I have been asked by my boss to stay late next Wednesday. Will that cause any conflicts with your schedule? What if he begins to ask me to stay late regularly? At what point will I decline?"

Part two of family council: The entire family. Second, the parents meet with all the other family members. During this part of the family council, each member of the family reports on their school assignments and upcoming tests, their extracurricular lessons or sports activities (such as the science fair on Thursday evening), and any other commitments where they will need rides (such as soccer practice), help making refreshments, or family support to attend a performance (such as back-to-school night). As issues are discussed, important items are written on the family calendar. It is often helpful to let each family member have a different-colored pen to write his or her commitments.

In addition, invite those involved to speak up early, ask for help, and detail progress they are making on personal projects. During this part of the family meeting, it is also useful to discuss the following:

- Commitments that require an adult to drive
- Commitments that require an adult to attend
- Commitments that require preparations
  - » An example is a wedding reception (gift, gas in the car, babysitter)
- Commitments that require adult supervision and involvement
  - » An example would be a science project

Work with all family members to speak openly and early about their need for support, transportation, or attendance to remove the panicky "I thought I told you about this" problem, especially if all commitments are recorded on an oversized wall calendar. Alternately, phone calendars can be coordinated.

Part three of family council: Parents and each child individually. Finally, the parents (both whenever possible) meet with each child separately. The children are asked about their individual lives, inquiries are made about issues with siblings or friends, and encouragement is given to bring up anything troubling them. Having a weekly time and place alone with their parents affords a child great security. No matter what the week has brought, there is a designated time for them to talk alone with Mom and Dad about their needs.

For example, if a youngster needs brownies for a school project on Wednesday, it is helpful to know about it as soon as he or she makes the commitment. Then brownie mix can be purchased and the brownies made on a calmer Tuesday afternoon instead of during a frenzied Wednesday before-activity marathon.

You will be amazed at the improvement in your family life, your relations with your spouse and children, and your feelings of control when you settle into a routine of having these regular family meetings.

The family council: Routines. It is most helpful to set a regular time aside each week (when the most family members will be home) to have a productive family council. You will be amazed how a weekly family council will change your life for the better.

SIMPLIFY AT ALL LEVELS

Many of you have "muddy bogs" in your routines, schedules, and habits. These are places where you approach life with too much chaotic spontaneity. As with all the other projects you are engaging in as you learn how to be organized, always look for ways to simplify your life. Here are four additional directives and their application to a regular family issue: laundry.

1. **Eliminate.** Eliminate from your wardrobe any difficult-to-keep-up or time-consuming pieces of clothing. An example would be a blouse that needs to be ironed before it can be worn.
2. **Reduce.** Reduce unneeded clothing items you have out and about by storing off-season items either in the back of your closet or in deeper storage areas of your abode.
3. **Postpone**. Postpone filling out your wardrobe (no matter what the fashion experts say!) and stick to about a dozen tried-and-true outfit combinations, especially during times of financial drought or emotional stress.
4. **Systemize**. Finally, systemize your professional and casual wardrobe by rotating through outfits so you will know what to wear tomorrow and even next week without having to think about it each morning.

Do you have other places where you can simplify, such as bill paying, mending, food management, or paperwork? If so, think through the four steps to simplification: eliminate, reduce, postpone, and systemize.

MAKE YOUR DAY LIKE A DANCE

Sometimes you begin your day frazzled and frustrated. This challenge can be overcome by approaching your day like a dance—and a lovely one at that.

Dress one level higher. One way to make your day more like a dance is to dress one level higher than your mood, so even when you are doing the laundry, tending to the garden, cleaning the dishes, or taking care of the children, you feel a little prettier. This small adjustment in dress will save you time, because you will tend to get at projects sooner, stay at them longer, and get them done quicker.

Practice a skill. Second, let's agree that there are certain personal home responsibilities you really don't like. It might be dusting, vacuuming, laundry, or dishes. It might even be all four of those things! To get your daily dance going, focus on learning the dance steps to one of these challenges. Sit down and write out why the organization skill is tough for you. Look at the chore and see what you can do to move from feeling panicked to finding a state of peace.

For example, let's tackle dusting. Dusting is hard because it is an "invisible" chore. It is only noticeable when it doesn't get done. It is also boring, so you might say to yourself, "I can avoid that chore for one more day." When you take time to look at this problem, you may realize that you don't have a good dusting glove and that touching dust with your fingers gives you the creeps. So you can add two dusting gloves to your shopping list and solve that problem. Then you may realize that you don't mind dusting the family room because there aren't a lot of flat surfaces to worry about, but the living room is nothing but trinkets that need to be picked up, dusted under, and put down again. By removing half the trinkets and rearranging them a bit, you could dust that room in half the time. Remember, small adjustments in your daily dance add up to minutes and hours over a week's time.

Look at your routines and see what you can do to make jobs easier to complete successfully. Do you need to buy better tools, paint a laundry wall to make the area cheerier, or organize toys so that daily cleanup is more pleasant?

Delete 10 percent of your commitments. When you dance through your day, there is an appropriate pacing and comfortable speed—meaning you are not trying to do too much in too little time. When you try to hurry, you often become frazzled. If you can downsize 10 percent of your pressures, there will be a significant improvement in your capacity to take care of your most important responsibilities. For example, you might say, "I'd be happy to read to you, but it would be better for me to just read this much before you go down for your nap."

So look at your laundry habits, your dish routines, your menu planning, or your child-care patterns and focus on one that is particularly frustrating and makes you frazzled. Ask yourself what you can do to dress a little nicer, to organize a little bit differently, and to delete a little bit here and there so the feeling of control can return to your life while you dance through your day.

START LESS; END EARLIER

As you become more organized, two important skills can aid in your journey. First, start less often, which means not starting up more in the beginning of the day than it is reasonable to finish by the end of the day. Second, learn to end earlier so you're refreshed for transition into the next part of your day. Let's look at examples of these two principles.

Let's say you have a complex summer ahead of you, including sponsoring a special-occasion breakfast. This would be a time when you don't want to make any major mistakes, leave things behind, or retrace your steps without difficult challenges. For things to work best for everyone, it is important to start less often. This means that during this focused time of preparation and packing, you wouldn't also start up projects that can wait, such as a new quilt that needs tying, three dresses for the community play, and two chocolate cakes for a church function.

Start less often also means "thinking it through" longer and not starting up more than you can finish in a reasonable time. As the stress rises and the complexity of difficult situations settles in, you will begin to worry. "Have I remembered everything? Will I have what I need when I need it? What will happen if I don't think clearly?"

When you move to the mode of "starting less," you can do a sort of mental role playing. In your mind, you can get up and dress yourself for the morning of the breakfast you are worrying about, thus confirming what clothes you will wear. You can walk through what tools and materials you might need for that day's activities, thus clarifying what you need to put aside for those needs. You can mentally walk through the sequence of the day's responsibilities, events, and pressures to see where you have holes in your thought processes, preparations, and possibilities. You can also decide what preparations are enough, because it is unlikely that you will be able to do much more before the big breakfast commitment takes place.

At times, you may have several pressing needs at once. During these more difficult times, you may want to prepare for all needs before the first begins, because there wouldn't be much time between events to mentally prepare for the next. In addition, remember to stop to rest before you are actually tired. As stated before, it is better to quit and rest before you reach the end of your energy. It helps to stop just shy of being fatigued. You will recover faster and have more resiliency to return to your project or prepare for the next demand.

Organize to start less often by thinking the event through carefully, writing down your thoughts, and then committing to starting only as many projects as you are likely to reasonably finish. As you work, watch for the first signs of fatigue and respond to them by resting and reviving. These two skills will help take the strain out of stressful seasons. When worry sets in, turn your mind to role playing and reasoning. It can make all the difference. And if you do leave something undone or take a short break to rest, at least you will be a more pleasant, thoughtful person to be around, and you will also feel more confident with each day's demands.

— ≫ 10 ≪ —

LAST MINUTE
TO LEISURELY

Life is almost always nicer when you start early.

- *Action project:* Purge and organize the laundry room
- Eliminate surprises
- Don't do more; do better
- Manage tardiness

Learning the skills of more leisurely living takes time and practice. Let's start with purging and organizing the laundry room. Then focus will move to preparing before, doing better, and adjusting your schedule when you will be late.

PURGE AND ORGANIZE THE LAUNDRY ROOM

"Setting up" the laundry room is very important for getting the job done right and efficiently. So let's get your laundry room purged of what doesn't need to be there and then set it up to expedite the laundry. How?

From the immediate area surrounding the washing machine and dryer, remove everything that doesn't have to do with washing, drying, and folding clothes. Wipe down flat surfaces, the washer (inside and out), and the dryer. Then purchase and gather tools to keep the laundry moving forward in a functional manner to the finish line. Here are some ideas:

Laundry room: Tools. Having the laundry room equipped with the right tools makes all the difference for a responsibility that is almost continuous in most people's lives.

Laundry soap. The laundry soap should be stored convenient to the washing machine. If you use dry soap and have a traditional top-loading washer, have the container top at the same level as the washing machine. This will make getting the dry soap into the washer easy and convenient. If you buy granulated laundry soap in bulk and stack three 40-pound buckets on each other with the top one open, it will be near the height of a traditional top-loading washer. Scooping is easy and there is less spilled soap. If you use liquid soap, store it convenient to getting the liquid into the washer with the minimum of steps.

If you have a front-loading washer that is set higher off the floor, getting the liquid soap into the right place without spilling may take some creativity. Work on it until the process is satisfactorily easy and efficient.

Lint waste. Place a small wastebasket convenient to the dryer for lint disposal. A spot at the same level as the traditional dryer top lets you pull off the lint, deposit it neatly, and keep the "dryer dust" to a minimum. It may not seem like a big deal, but if you have the wastebasket close by and you get into the habit of collecting the lint every time you use the dryer, you will also save money. Even with a higher mounted dryer, putting the lint in the wastebasket without moving much will also save a mess.

Clothes rod. Prepare a place to put dry clothes. This means a sturdy rod (usually a tension shower rod between two walls or a curtain rod hung from a chain connected to hooks screwed into the ceiling). It also means plenty of similarly sized and quality plastic hangers.

KEY CONCEPT: Standardization helps speed up organization. A good example is getting rid of hangers you might have inherited from the dry cleaner, hangers that came from the clothes store, and any other odd-sized, weak, or misshapen hangers. Purchase and use standardized, sturdy hangers. Your hands will get used to the feel and texture of the new hangers, and with practice, you can do the laundry faster and faster.

Folding table. You will also need a table, countertop, or even stacked boxes covered with a blanket for folding and stacking laundry. This folding table should be located near the dryer to be of the best use. You see, it doesn't have to be expensive or fancy to do the job well. (And sometimes the kitchen table or kitchen counter will have to serve as a folding table because of the location and size of your laundry room.) These laundry-expediting elements need to be there. Figure out a plan, make some purchases, and set things up.

Laundry containers. Collect or purchase containers for your clean and folded laundry. Having containers will confine the folded laundry until you can put it away yourself; or, better yet, have your family members (adult and children alike) help with this part of the process. Besides, having the laundry in containers and sharing the work takes a big job and cuts it down to manageable size.

Timer. Use a timer to remind you to move the laundry from the washer to dryer. Use it to time how long it takes to fold a batch of laundry. Use it when the children put their laundry away as a "who can get this job done fastest" motivator. It will help keep the laundry process moving and make it fun besides!

KEY CONCEPT: Consider purchasing tall, narrow kitchen wastebaskets as your laundry baskets. They take up less floor space both in the laundry room and in the bathroom and bedrooms.

Doing laundry may never be completely pleasant. But you can purge your laundry room to make the chore easier and set up the room to make doing laundry more expedient—which will let you get on to other, nicer household priorities!

Laundry: Systems. Once the laundry room is set up, the home manager working toward better organization figures out how to handle the consistent challenge of getting the never-ending, always-present, never-will-go-away laundry done. There are several useful skills and procedures to improve laundry routines.

Everyone helps. Those who contribute also appreciate! Everyone who wears clothes and can walk can help put laundry away. This increases gratitude for the main laundry doer and spreads out the work among all who live in the home. For example, have Rebecca put away the hand towels in the kitchen drawer, Fred put the main bathroom towels and washcloths away, and Milo put the car wash rags back in the garage box—in addition to each putting their own laundry away. You might want these laundry containers to also be the dirty clothes buckets/baskets for your bathrooms. This will save time and trouble as you (or your family helpers) collect the buckets from the bathrooms, get the wash done, put the wash away, and return the laundry containers to the bathrooms.

Reduce number of whites. Reduce the number of totally white items in your household (except, of course, special-occasion items such as boys' and men's white Sunday shirts). This is because most items will lose their whiteness with each washing. There will likely be mustard or catsup or dirt or chocolate to disfigure that beautiful white item. Yes, you can use bleach. But that is two steps back and only one step forward. Why complicate your life? Just keep to darker neutrals, patterns, and textured fabrics to save yourself a lot of time.

Laundry: Routines. Setting up good laundry routines is essential to keeping this chore done.

Frequency matters. Don't plan on a weekly laundry marathon. Plan to do laundry frequently, usually every day for the stay-at-home manager. Monday is for a batch of weekend clothes. Tuesday is for bath towels. Wednesday is for weekday clothes. Thursday is for bed sheets, and Friday is for another batch or two of weekday clothes.

The working person will find expediency in doing a load each evening around other responsibilities. A little laundry done more often keeps the laundry more done.

Do laundry in the background of your life. Always have the washer going while you are doing something else. Remember, a personal timer helps you get back to the laundry. Put the wash in, set the timer, and go off and do whatever. When the timer dings, move the wash to the dryer, set the timer again, and off you go again. When the timer dings, put the laundry on a counter and put in four to five minutes of "misery" while you hang items up or fold them neatly into your containers. Then off you go again to do whatever. This method makes laundry part of your daily dance, not an interruption to your daily routines.

Help adolescents do their own laundry. Rid yourself of laundry chores by teaching adolescents how to do their own laundry. Designate days when the washing machine will be available and incentives to get them to finish completely so the laundry room is available for others.

ELIMINATE SURPRISES

For a more organized life, attempt to reduce, if not eliminate, most surprises. Anticipate needs before they happen so you are prepared to respond when they do happen. Always look for ways to be prepared for the unexpected. Look for easy, permanent answers. Then apply these "ahead of your responsibilities" solutions as much as possible and in all circumstances. An example of preparing for unexpected company may be instructive.

There is no challenge quite like being caught unprepared, so why not have a plan for feeding unexpected company, either for a meal or for dessert? Sometimes the doorbell will ring and those standing on the step say, "Oh, we just happened to be close and we haven't seen you lately. May we come in?" When that happens, it is reassuring to be able to respond, "Sure. We are glad you are here. Come in and I'll prepare a small treat to share together."

To reply so confidently, you must prepare in two ways. First, you must plan beforehand what you will serve unexpected company. Second, you must have your pantry and refrigerator well stocked with items reserved for such needs. These items will be off-limits for regular family meals and will be used exclusively for unexpected company.

Stock the pantry and refrigerator. For example, your plans may include having cooked, cut-up, and frozen chicken pieces in the freezer for making a quick pasta casserole. You may keep frozen corn in the freezer and two cans of peaches on the back, bottom shelf of the refrigerator.

You may want to make up a batch of snickerdoodle cookies and freeze them. Then, when the unexpected company comes for dessert, you are well prepared to offer a cookie treat with a flourish.

Replenish again. When the "company food" is gone, it is time to add making snickerdoodles and cooking chicken to next week's chores. Add ice cream, canned peaches, and frozen corn to your grocery list too, so these items are also always at hand.

This is just one example of being the organized home manager you want to be. "I'm ready for you to come any time you want, and I'll have something special to feed you as we chat."

DON'T DO MORE; DO BETTER

Procrastination is a classic response when faced with a disagreeable, long, or difficult project. Sometimes the project is too big to easily comprehend and conquer. At other times, you may procrastinate because of fear or the anticipation of boredom. The secret is to break the project down, down, down into mini-steps that are both comprehendible and workable into your schedule.

Conquer your procrastination paralysis in a timely manner by thinking of one project you have procrastinated and would like to get done this next week. Then apply the following principles:

- **Make a list of mini-projects to get the big project done.** Seek to understand yourself better. Why do you avoid projects? Is it that you might make a mistake and ruin the project? Is it a lack of skills and not knowing who might teach you? Is it a matter of finances? Is it a lack of ever being in the right mood? Or is it that all projects take longer than you anticipate? Answer these questions, and then list the smaller projects that will help get the bigger project done.
- **Start on the first mini-project today.** Take the first small step today toward getting the project started. Plan when you will return to the project and what the next step will be.

- **Make the hard decisions necessary to get the project going.** Ask yourself, "What will be the worst possible result if I mess things up?" Then list alternative answers that can be pursued, like getting the cooperation of your spouse, asking for professional intervention, or tossing the project out.
- **Work through your fears.** Then tackle how you might be delaying a project because of its "fearfulness" or "boredom" factors. An example is handling the fear of painting a room. Yes, the paint may turn out to be the wrong color and you will have to start again. An example of boredom is hemming a pair of pants. So hem them while you listen to music. Alternatively, engage a friend to help with the project or do it during the highest energy time of your day to counter the challenge of a difficult or tedious project.
- **Find the next best time to do the next mini-project so it will not be so laborious.** Break projects down into mini-projects, make decisions, work past your fears of failure, understand the boredom elements, and set convenient times for working on the mini-projects necessary to complete the giant challenge. Get going now. When you learn to alleviate procrastination, you learn one more way to have an organized life.

MANAGE TARDINESS

The organized person is always trying to be timely, but occasionally situations arise when you will be late. How can you eliminate, or at least reduce, the stress you cause others because you don't always arrive in a timely manner? How do you relax when you know that you are going to be delayed? These principles can help:

- **Whenever possible, commit to "ish."** This means, "I will plan to meet you around 2 p.m., or 'two-ish,' if that will work with your schedule." This process allows you flexibility without causing problems for yourself or those you are meeting.
- **Make contact.** As soon as you realize you are going to be late, contact the person to let them know of your delay and set a new, approximate time of arrival. "I'm sorry, Marsha. I have been

caught in traffic and probably won't be arriving until sometime around 4:35. Will that timing still work for you?"

- **Set your bedroom clock four minutes fast.** Set the bedroom clock four minutes fast and the rest of the clocks in your home and vehicles two minutes fast. This will help others prepare a bit earlier and thus encourage timeliness. Arriving early doesn't waste time; it conserves energy and often accomplishes more. Early arrivers can network with business associates, visit with friends, and settle in without puffing, rushing, or feeling stressed. Simply put, try to live a bit early!

- **Address chronic lateness.** If you are a timely person and are working with a chronic late bird, tell the person, "The party is scheduled to start at 6 p.m. for everyone else, but for us the party is starting at 5:30 p.m." This will hopefully cause a laugh and bring the subject to the surface. Then it can be discussed and resolved. You might also say to a chronically late friend, "Mark, I'm starting to plan on you arriving about fifteen minutes after you tell me you'll arrive, because the last three times we have set a time to meet, you have shown up later than we had agreed. I know you may have hoped your tardiness would be overlooked because of our friendship, but it will help me plan if we work with 'ish' or you are more honest about when you plan to arrive, so I can better plan my schedule."

If you are running late, let others know. Tell others you will arrive "ish." Make contact as soon as you know you are running behind. Set clocks early and engage others in conversations about their repetitive tardiness. Others will respect you when you are usually on time. You can come to respect yourself when you keep to your committed timelines. You also face reality when you realize that sometimes you can't be in total control, and thus you call ahead about your anticipated tardiness.

And don't forget about the strange phenomenon with the traffic lights—they always seem to be red when you are running late and green when you are ahead of schedule.

—— » 11 « ——

AMBIGUITY
TO AMBITION

Make some
decisions just once.

- *Action project:* Purge and organize the garage and storage areas
- Increase storage capacity
- Engage in morning essentials
- Employ the law of firsts
- Buy more—less often

This chapter focuses on making better use of garage and storage areas, plus ambitious skills for saving large quantities of time and getting things done in a timely manner. First, let's continue your purging projects.

PURGE AND ORGANIZE THE GARAGE AND STORAGE AREAS

Purging and organizing the garage and storage areas will make more room for keeping things in order. While there never seems to be enough room for storage, you can employ techniques that will move your organization skills up one level and give you more time each day.

Garage and storage areas: Tools. As with other purging projects, you will need black and white garbage bags, a wastebasket, garbage containers, and a vehicle for loading items for the trash and thrift store. You are less likely to need the boxes labeled with each room because items in the garage are rarely misplaced from an inside location.

Garage and storage areas: Systems. Purging the garage begins with sweeping or spraying off the driveway. Because most concrete driveways have been divided into four sections, these areas can be used for purging and organizing the oversized items that often live in the garage. (1) The first driveway section can be for items that will be returned to the garage. (2) The second section can be for items that are useful but not needed and will be donated to charity. (3) The third section will be for not useful, not needed items that will end up at the dump. (4) The fourth section of the driveway is for items that belong elsewhere. So share and discard ruthlessly!

Clean out the garage by placing all items in one of the driveway sections. Remember that the garage is often the halfway house to the garbage because you know you don't need something anymore but might be afraid to completely remove it from your life.

Return to the garage items that belong in the garage, always looking for ways to hang oversized items or make use of your shelving.

Then, to keep items more organized, work on increasing your garage's capacity. You may need additional tools for hanging items from the ceiling and possibly more shelving units.

This purge and organization plan can also work in unfinished areas of a home, a storage shed, or other storage areas.

Garage and storage areas: Routines. To most effectively keep items moving out and away from your life, garages should be purged and organized about twice a year. This timing will make the garage more pleasant to enter each time you open the garage door.

INCREASE STORAGE CAPACITY

An effective, inexpensive way to increase garage or storage room capacity is the use of a simple box system.

Storage: Tools. Acquire or gather up to fifty sturdy and stackable containers. These can be plastic containers or boxes with lids. If you purchase plastic containers, clear containers with straighter sides and attached lids are useful because you can see what is inside, store more items in the same amount of space, and keep the lids close at hand.

Also needed are a 3" x 5" index card box, fifty index card dividers, and fifty or more lined 3" x 5" index cards. Number both ends of each box with a number, starting with 1 for the first box and moving toward 50 for the fiftieth box. Label each index card at the top right-hand corner with numbers 1 through 50. Note on the index card what you put in each box to keep track of the contents of that box. This helps with both physical and psychological organization, because the stacked containers are automatically an organized set regardless of their individual size and shape.

BOX 1

Christmas Tree Lights
Christmas Wreaths
Exterior Lights

Storage: Systems. Keep similar things together in your storage boxes. For example, keep Christmas items in boxes 1 to 10, camping supplies in boxes 11 to 15, and sporting equipment in boxes 16 to 20.

Label containers with large 1 to 50 numbers. Use sheets of cardstock to print up oversized numbers for both ends of 50 boxes/containers. Prepare the numbering system (the index cards) for fifty boxes too. Store the extra numbered cardstock sheets in the last-used box. When you add another storage container, you can take the numbered cardstock cards out and tape them to the front and rear of the boxes or place them inside the clear plastic containers.

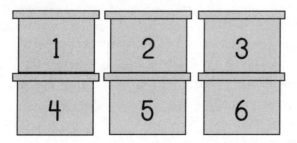

During some seasons, certain items will take more space than you may anticipate. Other times, the items will take less space. Either way, the box system works well. It also has the advantage of giving some items, such as Christmas gifts, the benefit of anonymity—especially if they are stored in mislabeled boxes.

Implement your storage tracking system. List what is in a container on the appropriately numbered index card and file the card numerically in the card box. Store spare index cards in the back of the index card box.

Storage: Routines. Implement a creative, permanent solution for storage needs in your garage or other storage areas, with or without any shelving. Start looking for lidded boxes and get that space organized. Then return to your storage boxes as needed for retrieval or to store more items.

As mentioned elsewhere, some items are best stored with direct labeling. As discussed in chapter 13, specific labeling is useful when storing children's clothing, shoes, underwear, and outerwear. As stated in chapter 5, direct labeling on storage containers is also useful when storing paperwork that needs to be kept long-term.

ENGAGE IN MORNING ESSENTIALS

In addition to reducing ambiguity in storage areas, you may be ambitious enough to try to make your mornings better. This might be compared to looking through a kaleidoscope. You have the same elements and the same problems every morning, but you can use new skills to manage life.

For example, if you had an unexpected late night, the morning after can be daunting. You might lose your pacing because the demands of the day seem to be sitting there ready to pounce as soon as you are up. Other times, the formal work day starts earlier than usual and you have to be ready to go before you're even really awake.

How do you keep up the essential habits (such as patterns of prayer, inspirational reading, exercising, and beautifying) that firmly launch you into a good day, even when you get a late start?

Pre-plan. When you know an upcoming morning is going to be hectic, your greatest tool is pre-planning. What simple outfit and shoes will fit your needs? In what order will you do your necessary routines? What tasks will you leave for later in the day? What will you substitute out or even eliminate?

For example, Rhonda was going to have an early, hectic morning. She chose a simple, easy-to-put-on outfit the night before that would meet her housecleaning needs and be useful when she shared lunch with an associate (minus the apron she would wear in the morning to keep her clothes clean and plus a scarf at her neck to dress up her outfit).

Keep to personal routines, just shorten them. When time is tight, still keep to your self-care routines, which might include exercise, prayer, inspirational reading, and journaling. Your morning prayer may have to be shorter and your exercise may have to be a brisk walk from your vehicle to the restaurant appointment and then back again—facilitated by parking an extra block away to accomplish your abbreviated exercise commitment.

Plan to read inspirational content from your phone while waiting for your associate, as that person is often a bit late and this would accommodate that part of your self-care routine. You could also make journal notes into a text to yourself if there was a further delay, and then make a complete journal entry when you arrive home.

Make yourself attractive enough. When time is tight, you can eliminate most of your fancy preparations and use your clothes to brighten your facial features in a natural way, and with the addition of an accessory, you would look nice enough.

You can prepare a simple breakfast and put the paperwork for your luncheon appointment in your vehicle.

Time-tight days can be managed successfully and methodically—and still include self-care routines. So be in charge of your days, your moods, and your accomplishments. Some mornings are messy, so have a plan of attack for all such mornings—especially those you can anticipate. Your personal self-care habits can still be a part of your routine, however abbreviated their time allotments may be!

EMPLOY THE LAW OF FIRSTS

The law of firsts suggests that when you do what is most important first, the rest of your life falls into place. Deciding the most important firsts in your life and then placing them at the forefront of your life also forms strong habits that add continued benefits.

For example, you might decide that the FIRST words in the morning are for a personal prayer or some meditation to increase your connection with the Divine.

You might plan that the FIRST reading of the day will be scriptures or other inspirational reading to stimulate your mind and soul.

You might decide to set aside the FIRST day of the week as a day of rest, a Sabbath that you keep holy.

You might choose to have the FIRST Sunday of the month be a fast day where you leave off eating and contribute the cost of three meals to the poor.

You might make your FIRST expenditure each month be a contribution to a church or charity, thus benefiting others even as you meet your own and your family's needs.

You might resolve that the FIRST items you will plan into your month will be times with immediate family members, obligations to your church or community, and projects that seem to be postponed month after month although they are a high priority.

Learning to live by prioritizing your time is one of the single best ways to keep on track. Decide what you will do first each day, what you will do first each week, and what you will do first each month. Try using the law of firsts and see if it doesn't align your deepest desires with the best use of your time.

BUY MORE—LESS OFTEN

You are probably familiar with the "this bottle feels empty" experience—when you know it is time to replenish. Or when the fuel tank's empty light comes on, the container of milk feels light, or your socks have a little hole in them. Often that thought is fleeting and you postpone addressing the issue. But having waited, you wait too long and then you are on empty! So it is essential to set your personal standards of replenishing. Then you never again need to face being on empty. Whether it is gas, checks or cash, stamps, socks, or medication, this is an organization problem you can solve in several easy steps.

Having replenishing standards and creating "sooner" habits will ensure you always have extra (and maybe even an overflow) in your life. Here's how:

- Review what is always running out.
- Decide when and how to initiate the replenishing process.
- Set up methods to remind yourself that it is TIME to replenish.

For example, you might say, "I will buy two rolls of stamps now and put a rubber band around the second roll as a reminder that I need to replenish. I will buy a new roll when I begin to use the second one."

"I will purchase two bags of socks the next time I buy socks for my children, my husband, or myself. I will keep the spare socks in the storage room so I will never run out of socks again."

"I will call for my prescription refill when I get down to my last ten pills and pick up the new prescription when I do my weekly grocery shopping."

Standards for replenishing will help life run itself a little smoother. You will feel more organized when the sock gets a hole, because you can simply go to your stash to replenish. When your gas hits the quarter-full mark, you know it's just about time to look for a station. When the medication bottle begins to feel empty, it is time to call in a refill prescription. With every new skill, you are moving toward a more orderly life!

By setting replenishing standards and then sticking to them (as best as you can), your mind moves forward to a new and safer place. Work toward greater organization by being well stocked up.

Then, as a next step, why not go shopping as infrequently as once a year for those nonfood items you regularly use? There are many benefits to reducing the number of times you visit a store for sundries, paper products, and toiletries. Every eliminated trip saves time, hassle, decision-making, and money. Why not make a yearly trip to the store and purchase all the nonfood items you need for a whole year? It is easy and ever so time saving.

Conduct an inventory. How do you begin? In addition to reviewing receipts for the past three months, do an inventory of the nonfood items in your cupboards and closets. As you walk through the house, list every item that you regularly use and which could potentially be purchased once a year. For instance, you can buy toilet paper, facial tissues, over-the-counter medications, ziplock bags, and many other items just once a year. It is helpful to note on your inventory the size of each item you regularly use. This allows for comparison shopping. Then note how many of each item you have on hand and how many you estimate you will need for a full year.

The first time you do this, it will be a guessing game at best, but with practice you will get good at knowing how much of each item you use in a year's time.

Estimate the cost. Estimate how much each item will cost and note that on your inventory. With practice, you will get better at knowing what a good price is, but for now a reasonable estimate will do. Now you are ready to go shopping.

Cherry-picking. The first time you do "once a year" shopping, you may find it best to cherry-pick. This practice allows you to eliminate a lot of shopping while getting the best possible prices. Take your inventory and visit three of your favorite stores. (As an alternative, you can visit your favorite stores online to check prices there too.)

At the first store, price each item you are interested in buying and record that price on your inventory. Go to the second store and do the same pricing, and then visit the third store and do final pricing. Circle the best prices at each of the three stores and make the purchases you desire at the third store. Then return to the first store and buy the items, in the quantities you need, that are cheapest at that store. Do the same with the second store. You have now purchased items at each store at the cheapest prices.

Most items that have been purchased should be date-stamped. This can be done with a permanent marking pen or with a date stamp and stamp pad. Alternatively, you can use a yellow highlighter to set off expiration dates. This allows you to confidently rotate your items when you make next year's purchases.

Store at home. Don't worry about having enough storage space before you shop. Just go and buy. When you get home, you will be surprised how easy it is to fit some of the items in this cupboard and some under that bed and others on this shelf. When you are done storing the items, sit down and be amazed. You will find that during the next year you will have a lot more time for doing things beside buying sundries because these are now safely stashed in your home "store."

— » 12 « —

FLUSTERED
TO FINISHED

Employ skills to amplify personal and familial functioning.

- ***Action project:*** Purge and organize closets, drawers, and cupboards
- Learn to finish completely
- Retire from putting out others' fires
- Keep little things little

This chapter offers more ideas about moving from being flustered to living in a personal world of finishing. How can you move from flustered to finished? First, purge and clean out all the remaining closets, drawers, and cupboards in your home. Then learn how to put everything back in its home, finish projects completely, teach others independence skills, and work at keeping little things little. Let's start with making your closets, drawers, and cupboards more storage friendly.

PURGE AND ORGANIZE CLOSETS, DRAWERS, AND CUPBOARDS

Cleaning out the rest of your closets, drawers, and cupboards may take some time, but it is one of the important ways a home manager begins to feel in complete control. Certain procedures make this project much nicer to contemplate, too, so let's go to work!

Closets and cupboards: Tools. The tools needed for purging the rest of the closets and cupboards are similar to those used when purging the other rooms in the home: boxes (labeled with the names of other rooms in the house), white garbage bags for items to share, black garbage bags for items to discard, and a wastebasket for small discard items.

Take all the items from a closet shelf, a closet rod, or the closet floor and place them aside while you clean out the closet. Do the same as you clean your cupboards and drawers. Sort the items three ways, putting useful and needed items back in your closet, cupboard, or drawer. Items that go elsewhere go into your boxes. Items to be shared or discarded go into the appropriate white or black garbage bags.

These same tools, systems, and routines can be applied to every cupboard, drawer, and closet you want to purge and organize. Continue to practice your skills of purging and organizing. As you do so, also employ the additional skills mentioned in this chapter.

LEARN TO FINISH COMPLETELY

There is great power in learning to finish. Surprisingly, as you become aware of this principle, you may find that you routinely live in a rather unfinished state. Practice finishing to save time and help tighten your organizational functionality.

There are several kinds of finishing: the standards of finishing in daily habits, the skill of finishing yourself, and the ability to finish bigger projects.

Standards of daily finishing. Making decisions as a family about daily "finishing" standards can take a lot of stress out of life. When is a meal finished? When is the laundry finished? When is housework finished?

Work with family members to set up standards that the whole family can support and practice to finish.

Skill of finishing yourself. Additional personal finishing skills are helpful in modeling finishing habits. Do you completely put away the groceries after a trip to the store? Do you finish at your desk and put away your paperwork when you leave that area? Do you hang up your coat and put away your gloves when you come in from a walk?

Finishing bigger projects. The challenge with finishing is that you are likely to start something, abandon the project to start another project, and then put that second project aside before it's done to begin a third. As the day proceeds, you continue to start other things and then give those projects up before you get far with them. Your whole environment can be full of unfinished projects, paperwork, and purchases.

The way to conquer this problem is to practice finishing, or at least bring your projects to a finishing place and put them away in a timely manner before other pressures descend.

For example, if you are cleaning out a cupboard, you will want to finish this project or bring this project to a place of partial finishing before the children get home from school and need help with snacks and homework. Then you can return to the project later in the evening or the next day.

To practice, make a list of three home projects that need finishing. List the particulars needed to get each of these projects finished and spend the time necessary doing just that: finishing!

RETIRE FROM PUTTING OUT OTHERS' FIRES

Another useful skill is to stop putting out others' fires. Solving others' problems, their fires, can be frustrating. Sometimes you commit past your capacity, other times you feel socially obligated, and still other times you may be intimidated about having to help—or else. Let's get some boundaries set and return to feeling in control again.

How can you get a grip and what can you do to regain a semblance of order? There are specific steps for handling feeling confused, reducing intimidation as stress mounts, and regaining a semblance of control.

Stop and ponder. When you feel like you are just "putting out fires" instead of continuing with whatever you're doing, take a few moments to stop and ponder. By stopping and figuring out what's going on, you can get a grip. Whose problem is this, anyway, and how can I help them solve it instead of solving it myself?

You may be a bit more overwhelmed than usual because the laundry is overly large and your adolescent's clothing has stains that look difficult to get out, or maybe you are confused because your son hasn't decided what menu he wants for his birthday dinner later in the week, or maybe you are feeling stressed because three close friends are having differences and you are in the middle. When you feel overwhelmed, figure out what you need to do from that point forward to let others solve their own problems.

Create an action plan. If you are feeling misused, create a plan of action. "Okay, I'm in a confused state. It feels like I'm handling too many fires today. Exactly what will I do to get back to a place that's more peaceful, where I feel more in control?" "OK, I am going to teach Rob how to get the grass stains out of his jeans." "I'll ask Eli to write up his birthday menu and give it to me by tomorrow." "I'll email my three friends, politely withdraw from my involvement, and suggest they get together for lunch soon to talk directly to each other about solving their issues." Making plans of action will help manage your life in the middle of a "fire season."

Face your increasing stress by stopping, pondering, and planning. "What is mine to solve? What fires belong to other people?" Then create a plan of action to give others back their own problems to solve. You don't have to put out other people's fires anymore.

You will likely find that when you withdraw from being all things to all people, the world survives quite nicely without your "immediate" attention—and hopefully others will begin to put out their own fires.

Teach self-reliance. Teach your family members to come to you with both their problems *and* with possible solutions to those problems. This invitation helps them realize that their problems are their own to solve. Such a stance will help them on their way to independence and self-reliance—and save you time!

KEEP LITTLE THINGS LITTLE

Sometimes your problems seem to grow out of proportion. Small problems seem to balloon, and you begin to feel emotionally overwhelmed. Employ the following methods to keep little things little.

Make a list of what's on your mind. As soon as you realize you are feeling overwhelmed and emotionally unable to cope, sit down with a piece of paper, fold it in half lengthwise, and dump your troubles onto the left side of it (initially skip a line between all entries). This will help calm you down!

On the left side of the paper, list everything that comes to mind, from the leaky faucets to the running toilets, to the need to fix dinner for company on Friday evening to buying a birthday present for that invitation that arrived over the weekend. Dump it all out, especially your feelings. The list might include your guilt at having missed sending birthday greetings to your close friend, the expensive produce that tasted terrible, and frustration because your favorite pair of jeans has a new hole in the wrong place.

List possible answers. On the right side, note what you can do to address or solve the problems listed on the left-hand side of the list, who you can approach to find answers to your needs, how you will handle the situation next time so you aren't embarrassed, and on and on. Some of your right-hand list entries will say, "There is nothing I can do." Knowing what can be done and what must be left alone is the first step to keeping little things little. (See "Emotional Dump List" form in the appendix.)

EMOTIONAL DUMP LIST	
What's on My Mind?	What I Can Do about It!

(This procedure differs from that described in chapter 4 and chapter 6. Here you are managing and resolving more emotionally focused needs. In chapter 4, you learned how to use a to-do list to get ready early and set priorities. In chapter 6, you returned to using a to-do list to reduce your immediate, pressing responsibilities, diminish stress, and proceed with more lineal living.)

KEY CONCEPT: You always want to move from problems to finding solutions and to regaining control again.

Decide where to use your energy. Take this list of what is bothering you and then plan how to tackle these sometimes emotionally overwhelming demands. In other words, use the right-hand list to employ the skills taught earlier in this book about prioritizing.

Attach "A," "B," or "C" priority letters to each item on the right-hand list. Decide what "A" items to do on what days, what "B" items to leave until later, and what "C" pressures would be put aside for some distant "slower" period of your life. The notations on the right side of your list will guide your schedule as to which projects will receive your attention today, tomorrow, during the rest of the week, and into the upcoming month. Some items will have to be postponed until the next month, and a few even longer. And some may never get done—because there is nothing to be done. The important principle is that you decide how you want to respond. Then, motivation to get up and get going often returns.

Schedule longer launch and landing periods. After you have set your "A," "B," and "C" priorities, add longer launch and landing periods to your calendar. While stress sometimes comes because of an emergency, it more often rises slowly and catches you in a hurricane of too many big projects, major activities, and other adventures. It is up to you to create or expand the "launch" and "landing" time bubbles so you can gear up successfully, come down and de-stress, get back to your regular routines, and otherwise "return" with appropriate pacing.

Remember, you are always going to be pushed by others to the very limit of what you will allow. If you allow less chaos, taking more time for "launching" and "landing," you will still be respected and will be able to respond better because you are handling your pressures and responsibilities in a more orderly, "I can do this and this and no more, no sooner than this" method.

Re-emerge. After this short respite, you can usually re-emerge into your life. When you do, take a moment to notify those around you that things may need to be a little different: "No, I am not going to go to that meeting; yes, I am planning on a simple dinner; no, I won't be able to wash those special pants until Saturday; yes, I would appreciate some babysitting help this evening; yes, I could use help folding and putting the wash away, getting a load of dishes going, and sweeping the kitchen floor."

Remember, it is up to you to make life work for you and your family, in your workplace, and all throughout your life. You are in charge of taking back your life and making sense of it, over and over again. Take a break and recalibrate to bring answers and motivation back. Then, when you get going again, life suddenly seems to turn around and you can smile!

—— » 13 « ——

WHINER TO WINNER

Give them
a more
organized
future.

- **Action project:** Purge and organize children's bedrooms
- Teach organization words
- Teach competency
- Teach return and report
- Teach self-initiative

If you are a parent, you are probably eager for your children, no matter their ages, to grow up as strong, independent, fully functioning adults. You want them to have self-initiative, to be hardworking, honest, and diligent. You want them to stop whining and learn to be organizational winners. And, yes, children of all ages are capable of and will benefit from small, significant opportunities to learn organization skills. In this chapter, let's work first with your children, as appropriate, to purge and organize their rooms. Then let's look at four organization principles and review examples to illustrate each skill.

PURGE AND ORGANIZE CHILDREN'S BEDROOMS

Purge your children's rooms using the same tools, systems, and routines as taught in chapter 4 about the master bedroom and chapter 12 about closets, drawers, and cupboards. Every cleaned-out closet or cupboard becomes another more functional "tool" in your home. Let's make children's bedrooms more organized too.

Youth clothing needs. Sadly, children's and adolescents' clothing needs seem to always be in flux. Even after you purge your children's bedrooms to meet current clothing needs, you need to figure out what on-hand clothing you can use for the upcoming season's needs and what you will need to purchase to fill out each child's or teenager's wardrobe.

Most projects, especially a big one like this, are best done in small steps. Your goal is to get all the useful and needed clothing back in the closet, but it is also to get all those extra clothes out of their bedrooms and safely given away or put away for the next child or given away to someone else.

Prepare clothing storage containers. It is best to purchase, find, or collect containers that will be useful for long-term storage. As stated before, storage containers should be stackable (when empty or full), sturdy, and clean. If you purchase plastic containers, those that are "semi-opaque" make it easier to see the contents inside and allow for easy labeling of the boxes (with large words printed on sheets of cardstock put inside both ends of the containers). This storage container investment will be well worth the trouble because you will be able to use these containers over and over until your children are grown.

Gather or purchase enough similar boxes or plastic bins to label three boxes for each age and gender of your family members. Generally, one box of tops, one box of bottoms, and one box for accessories provide a reasonable amount of clothing storage for most children. This means that a family with a one-year-old boy would have three boxes.

Each box is labeled with gender, age, and type of clothing. For example, Boy–1 TOPS, Boy–1 BOTTOMS, and Boy–1 ACCESSORIES. This last box holds shoes, boots, and other accessories. Again, you will need three boxes for each age of each gender. These boxes can act as your initial stashes as you sort, find, and make decisions about clothing needs. If you have a boy who is two, then the boxes will be labeled Boy–2 TOPS, Boy–2 BOTTOMS, and Boy–2 ACCESSORIES.

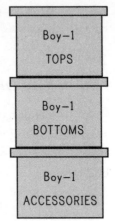

Out-of-season clothes that are useful but not needed for the time being (meaning they don't currently fit any of your children) should be stashed in additional labeled boxes or containers. For example, with boys: Boys–3 BOTTOMS, Boys–3 TOPS, and Boys–3 ACCESSORIES.

Or with girls: Girls–4 BOTTOMS, Girls–4 TOPS, and Girls–4 ACCESSORIES. Sometimes you will also need a Girls–4 SKIRTS/ DRESSES box as your girls begin to enjoy variety in their wardrobes. Remember, you will prepare these boxes for the ages of all your family members. This makes retrieving items easier and putting clothing into storage easier too.

Suggesting so many boxes may seem over-the-top because of your limited storage capacity. If you are in that category, you can use one box for every two years of age (and store the clothes accordingly) or just one box for every year (eliminating the separation between tops, and bottoms, and accessories). It just makes for a little more hassle when getting clothes out of the boxes.

Consider other needs. You might also consider gathering containers and labeling them for the following:

- Socks
- Underwear
- Swimwear
- Seasonal accessories
- Costumes

These items are easier to store separately because you will be in these containers a lot and sizes for these are often not as important.

Use clear ziplock bags, for example, labeled "Boys–1, Boys–2, Boys–3, Boys–4," etc., for the boys' socks box and keep the appropriately sized, folded socks inside the labeled ziplock bag inside the socks box. This allows you to buy socks on sale and have a place to keep them until they are needed. You can use the same method for storing underwear, taking advantage of sales whenever you can.

KEY CONCEPT: While variety is wonderful, similar-color socks for one age saves sorting time in the laundry room. If you have sons, for instance, you might have gray socks for your three-year-old boy, white socks for your four-year-old boy, and white socks with stripes for your five-year-old boy.

Do a formal clothing inventory. Do a formal clothing inventory mid-summer and again during the winter holidays. These inventories allow you to see what new clothing items need to be acquired because of growth and what clothing your children want to purchase—and they also let you take advantage of seasonal clothing sales. Plus, it helps family members settle into a twice-a-year clothing purchase pattern, which also saves time and money.

You may want to prepare a simple **School Clothing Inventory** you can use again and again to expedite this process, keep the budget in tow, and help you buy just enough clothing for your needs. (See "School Clothing Inventory" in the appendix.) List the following on the inventory:

- Number on hand
- Number needed
- Number to purchase
- Budget
- Number purchase
- Actual cost

KEY CONCEPT: As mentioned in chapter 5, set up permanent lists or forms for any household projects you will repeat again and again; it is a great way to save time.

As you sort and store clothing, it is easy to take this inventory. Then you can shop with your printed inventories, which will act as your shopping list. Finally, you can mend, alter, and otherwise label the clothing so it can be useful for a while longer.

Finally, you can put clothes that are not currently needed in boxes and store them safely but conveniently in your garage or storage areas. (Note that storing clothing in this way uses a different method than the general storage system using numbered boxes detailed in chapter 11. It is also different from the labeled box system for storing paperwork discussed in chapter 5. This is because you want to retrieve the clothing box you need with the greatest of ease.)

Have a massive organizing party. You may find that you would like to have your children share an afternoon at a neighbor's house (and then return the favor for your neighbor) the next time you tackle sorting and storing clothes. You may want to neglect your ringing phone and doorbell. With focus and hard work, you can empty your children's closets and bedrooms ONE at a time and sort clothes into your containers (which you might lay out around the edges of your master bedroom for convenience). After you have sorted through the clothing, pick out outfits that you will have your children use right now and return them to closets and drawers.

Keep clothing items available to your children to a minimum. You can rotate more clothes out when you need, but for the most part, keep more of your clothes in storage. Younger children don't need a lot of clothes to be happy. They have their minds on a lot of other things, so keep it simple. (But you will want to have a dress-up box handy for those creative moments.)

Store the extras away. After you have chosen which clothes to keep out, put the rest of the clothes into the containers, close them up, and store them where they will be convenient and yet out of the way (usually in the basement, storage area, or garage). When the seasons change, school begins again, or you find a child is rapidly moving out of the clothes they are wearing, head off to your storage containers, storing the undersized items and pulling out new, larger clothing.

Prepare a "To Be Stored" container. It is useful to have one of your easy-to-get-to storage containers labeled "To Be Stored." Thus, when you are in a rush or receive clothing that needs to be sorted and stored, or know it is time to put something away but don't have the mental energy to store it at that moment, you have a temporary stopping place for these items. It helps keep all those excess clothes confined and conquered!

Set up a clothing storage system for your children and you will find that everything will be easier at your house, from cleaning up children's rooms to doing their laundry.

TEACH ORGANIZATION WORDS

You can initiate teaching organization skills to any children who have basic language skills. Start with four-letter words, because they are especially effective and easy for children (of any age) to remember.

Four-letter organization words include COME, MOVE, TOSS, HOME, and DONE.

Of course, as with any other set of skills, teaching children about organization has a first step. It is: COME.

This skill is usually taught soon after children can easily and independently walk. By this time, children are also interacting regularly with adults. The goal is to get children to come to you when asked in a soft voice, and you want them to come the first time they are asked. The steps in this skill are: the asking, the response, movement/non-movement by the children, and the successful accomplishment of the task.

The asking. As a parent, you can set precedence by always speaking to your children in a low, kind tone. A significant change in tone or volume should only be used when there is immediate danger to the children. Otherwise, children need to know that they are emotionally safe with you. There will be consequences, but there will not be anger (at least not often).

Getting angry with children teaches them that responding to life includes responding with anger. The more you are in control when you speak, the more you are teaching your children how to be in control when they speak. The parental skill here is to talk in a friendly, imploring voice.

If children are sitting and you say COME, the goal is to get them to look up, get up, and move. If they are standing, the goal is to get them to look up and move (toward you).

Work with one child at a time when beginning this skill set. Gumdrops (or another type of treat) in your pocket can act as a motivator. There is nothing like sweetness at the end of success to solidify standards.

The response. The children will probably give you some indication that they have heard you. Watch carefully and make eye contact as you do the asking so you are sure there has been a response.

Movement/non-movement. Children do three things when asked to COME. They will come toward you, they will ignore you, or they will walk (and sometimes run) away from you. Often this running away is accompanied by laughter, which means that the children want to play with you.

Of course, there are many variations, including coming and then stopping, going and then returning, and ignoring and then responding.

The accomplishment of the task. Children who do come when asked should be rewarded generously with praise, touch, and more praise. (However, this usually doesn't happen the first time you teach this talent.) Learning this skill will take some time and many repetitions. Often, as a parent, you might feel upset and unhappy when your children don't respond to your request the first time you make it. Remember, it will take many times of trial and error, starting and stopping, to teach any child to come when called.

Thus, this skill is best worked at in the confines of a peaceful home, with plenty of time to practice. Here is a possible set of interactions:

John is playing with his trucks on the family-room floor. You settle into a chair about three feet from him.

"John, please come here."

John looks up and then returns to his toys.

"John, please come here. I have a gumdrop and a hug for you."

John looks up, sees the candy, stands up, and begins to come. Then he becomes distracted and picks up another toy.

"John, please come here. See the gumdrop is green. I'm eating one. They are good."

John stands up again and comes all the way to you.

"Wow, John! You obeyed me. You came when I asked you to come. Here is a green gumdrop for you and a big hug for coming when I asked you to. Thanks!"

Time after time, day after day, parents and children repeat this type of scenario. The goal: They are asked to come, they come. Then follows your praise, reward, and touch.

Sometimes children will run in the opposite direction. Practice your response in the safety of your home with plenty of time so you will have an established routine when asking children to come to you in a more public setting. The following might be a possible scenario:

"John, please come here."

John looks up, knowing the game well by now, and stands up. He laughs and heads in the opposite direction.

(Don't get angry. Keep your head. Play with the player.)

Run lightly after John, pick him up, and hug him.

"John, I said 'please come here' and you ran in the opposite direction. I love you. You played the game in reverse. Let's try again. You be the daddy, and I'll be the little boy. You ask me to come and I'll go away."

Then play this routine out:

"John, now let's play the game in double reverse. You ask me to come and I'll come with a gumdrop for you."

Finally, play this scenario out:

"John, now let's play the game with you coming to me. I'll be the daddy and you'll be my son, John. I'll ask you to come. You come and we'll eat a gumdrop together."

Practice with your children until they know to come the first time they are called, every time they are called, and immediately after they are called. (Soon, they will grow mature enough to ask if they can come "in a few minutes," but initially, the skill is to get the child to obey and come *now*.)

When this skill is in place, it lays a sure foundation for other organization skills a child needs to function at a high level. When a child can COME, he can more easily MOVE (such as pushing in a chair after meals), TOSS (put an item in the wastebasket), know where HOME is (and put toys away where they belong), and understand DONE (meaning that all chores must be worked at until they are finished). From here, you can adapt your teaching to an expanded organization skill vocabulary you would also like to have in your home.

TEACH COMPETENCY

Teaching children to keep to standards of acceptable conduct, especially when it comes to cleaning up, is a good first step in saving time. This entails a sequence of tasks that include job competency, return and report, and self-initiative.

Let's start with the skill of competency and use an illustration of a small area that consistently becomes disorganized: the family vehicle. Training your children to help with cleaning out the car upon arriving home is an excellent way to encourage competency in organization.

Teach your children what "neatening" the car means to you (trash gone, food remains picked up, shopping bags to the house, coats gathered, etc.). This training is best done after running errands and by stopping about one block from your home, when there is ample time for explaining the new plan and answering their questions.

Divide the car up and invite each child to clean the section where they are sitting. It is likely you will have to continue to do the deep cleaning until your older children or teenagers can be taught to do this as part of their Saturday jobs, but all your children can easily be responsible for their personal belongings and for cleaning up a section of the car. During this first training session, have the children identify the personal items they will need to retrieve and what will need to be cleaned up in their assigned section of the car.

For example, Ron (who is four) would be in charge of bringing his personal belongings (gloves and coat) into the house and also to pick up the stray Cheerios and empty ziplock bag on the floor of the car in front of his car seat.

Individual responsibilities. It is likely that you would personally be in charge of the driver's seat, have the older children in charge of the passenger side of the front and middle seats, and have younger children in charge of areas around their car seats. Really young children can be assigned as Mommy's or Daddy's car helpers.

Family meeting regarding competency. Within a few days, have a short family meeting to explain the new system again and then implement this routine again the next time you almost arrive home. Don't drive into the garage, but stop on the driveway or even in the street and remind the family that before they climb out of the car, they are to finish their car chores. Even if they have to make two trips to do it right, it is to be done before they begin other projects at home.

This type of personal organization and responsibility is a great way to help children discover who is making the mess and who is responsible for cleaning up the mess, as well as to help keep this significant "minihome" in your life neat and functional.

TEACH RETURN AND REPORT

Your capacity to help children is shored up by realizing that all children benefit from the concept of return and report. This means that after a child has received a job, such as cleaning up their area of the car, they are to come to you and indicate they are finished with the job. Before they are free to leave, check to make sure the job is done right. This pattern will be repeated until the child shows himself or herself to be repeatedly competent at the job. Then children can be told they need not "return and report" again unless they don't do the job completely in the future.

TEACH SELF-INITIATIVE

A great time to begin introducing self-initiative skills is when you organize for children's jobs. There are several important concepts to consider as you approach jobs for your family members.

- **Tell.** Remind children about the family's daily neatness standards for their bedrooms. This is their first daily responsibility. Then suggest they choose additional daily chores that would suit them best from a list of potential jobs. Children benefit from learning a variety of household job skills. What household skills will you teach them? When will this teaching take place? During summer vacation, will they be in charge of making one general-use room neat each day? Will they dust, vacuum, and clean another room once a week? Will they have chores in your yard and have a garden portion to weed, water, and harvest? Will they learn to cook, maybe at lunchtime?

KEY CONCEPT: After deciding who will do what and how much each person will be responsible for, take time to describe the job completely. It is helpful if children in your family are each involved in dusting part of the house, vacuuming a room, cleaning part of the bathrooms, and cleaning part of the kitchen. They should be involved with doing the laundry, meal preparation and cleanup, and yard work.

- **Teach.** Teach them how to do the jobs so they will be done to an acceptable standard. Non-school time offers more time for instruction, more leisure for checking to make sure jobs are done correctly, and more capacity for personal patience without a lot of outside pressures. Introduce simple, repetitive jobs, include the standards desired, teach the methods required, and show them that practice makes jobs go faster.

KEY CONCEPT: Take plenty of time at the beginning to teach them the right way to do each job. If this teaching is not done appropriately, there will be frustration, sullenness, and disappointment all through the duration of doing this job.

- **Time.** Use a timer as the children do each job to show them how long the job takes. Then repeat the timed sequence as they do the job again and again to show they can get better each time they do their chores with focus and diligence. Time them at their jobs for several days. This helps introduce the concept that "if you do a job repetitively and are diligent, you can not only do it better, but, at the same time, you can do it faster."

KEY CONCEPT: It is not as important that children work for long hours during summer vacation. Quite the contrary, have smaller time commitments for younger children and reasonable periods of work for older children. It doesn't take much time to keep the home in order, the laundry done, the meals prepared, and the yard work finished if everyone has their individual responsibilities and is competently completing them.

- **Use S. I.** Introduce the concept of S. I., which is the concept of self-initiative. There is great satisfaction in doing a job without being asked and with an extra level of excellence.

KEY CONCEPT: Over and over, speak to your family regarding self-initiative. You will find that your children will soon be their own best taskmasters. Set up a system for rewarding self-motivation. For instance, have special colored drinking glasses at dinner for those members of your family who do their chores during the day without being asked. In other words, when they show self-initiative, let everyone know about it. Such recognition becomes a symbol of their achievements and willingness to cooperate.

Each time a child begins a job of his own initiative, completes a job well, and receives sufficient praise for his work, he becomes more confident of finding his place in the world. One of the best gifts you can give your children is teaching them the values, wonders, and feelings of a job well done. And with their help, you will have a lighter load for maintaining the home, cleaning the yard, and keeping up with the laundry.

Remember, parenthood is not a popularity contest. You are in charge to make the rules, provide the opportunities to work and learn, and protect a daily quiet time for reading and personal projects. Take a few minutes to formulate your plans and then teach them useful organization skills!

Choose the skills you would like them to learn, teach them diligently, let them retain their favorite jobs during the school year, and then repeat the process again with more difficult and complex jobs the next summer. Soon your children will become quite adult-like. They may complain occasionally, but they will also be looked up to by their peers as they become independent, dependable, and competent.

As a side note, if your family is on a year-round school schedule, these same skills could be taught during off-school weeks. It will be more difficult to establish a routine cadence because the vacation times will be shorter, but it is important for children to be responsible for part of the household maintenance.

—— » 14 « ——

CONCLUSION

Everyone who strives to be organized can be likened to floral gardeners. Initially, the flower garden plot has to be purged of weeds, debris, and rocks. The garden then has to be organized in preparation for planting. This may include decisions about tree and bush placement, enrichment of soil, placement of sprinklers, and preparation of holes for plants or rows for flower seeds. Then the gardeners move forward with planting.

After the initial purging, organizing, and planting, the gardeners frequently return to maintain the obtained organization by watering and weeding—and sometimes the replanting of plants and seeds. This garden maintenance becomes part of the dance of the gardener's daily and weekly routines.

The hope is that the gardeners planted more chrysanthemums than daisies, especially if they want to have a garden filled with brilliant, full blooms.

You, too, can purge and organize your life's garden. Then you can maintain the organization you have obtained, even as you strive for better organization skills. If you occasionally feel discouraged about all the time and energy organizing is taking, remember that once you have acquired your tools, set up your systems, and figured out your routines . . . well, you are on your way to a whole life of more free time.

For more than thirty years, I have helped people get their personal lives and homes organized. I have often returned a second time to help them retain their newfound organization and help them personalize their organization skills. And, sometimes, I have returned a third, fourth, and fifth time to help them stay organized. Organization is not just a goal; it is also a process. Some days you'll feel on top of your organization skills. Other days you will feel frustrated and distraught. Remember this saying when the days are rough: It does take a lot of work to be organized, but it takes a lot more work to be disorganized.

If you stay dedicated to the principles in this book, your life's garden can be full of chrysanthemums. Yes, you have to take the time to get organized. Yes, you have to practice being organized. And yes, you will have to remain motivated to staying organized. But if you keep practicing your skills and adjusting to new organizational challenges, you can reclaim up to ninety minutes per day, every day, to pursue projects that you desire.

—— » Happy organizing! « ——

—— » Appendix « ——

ORGANIZATION FORMS

Various forms spoken about in this book have been included in this appendix to help you get more organized. They may be copied, scanned, and reprinted as is for personal use. You may also change them up to meet your individual needs. However, they may not be scanned, copied, or reprinted for professional or business use.

There are six forms included in this appendix. They are referenced by (1) the chapter where the form is explained in the book, (2) the title of the form, and (3) the appendix page number where the form is found.

PURGING PLAN FORM

| EEE PLAN—EVERYTHING OUT, ESSENTIALS IN, EXTRAS GONE |

ROOM	ROOM	ROOM

SHELVES, DRAWERS, CLOSETS	SHELVES, DRAWERS, CLOSETS	SHELVES, DRAWERS, CLOSETS
☐ _____	☐ _____	☐ _____
☐ _____	☐ _____	☐ _____
☐ _____	☐ _____	☐ _____
☐ _____	☐ _____	☐ _____
☐ _____	☐ _____	☐ _____

ROOM	ROOM	ROOM

SHELVES, DRAWERS, CLOSETS	SHELVES, DRAWERS, CLOSETS	SHELVES, DRAWERS, CLOSETS
☐ _____	☐ _____	☐ _____
☐ _____	☐ _____	☐ _____
☐ _____	☐ _____	☐ _____
☐ _____	☐ _____	☐ _____
☐ _____	☐ _____	☐ _____

ROOM	ROOM	ROOM

SHELVES, DRAWERS, CLOSETS	SHELVES, DRAWERS, CLOSETS	SHELVES, DRAWERS, CLOSETS
☐ _____	☐ _____	☐ _____
☐ _____	☐ _____	☐ _____
☐ _____	☐ _____	☐ _____
☐ _____	☐ _____	☐ _____
☐ _____	☐ _____	☐ _____

FAMILY IDENTIFICATION FORM

Last Name _____

First Name _____

Date _____

	Thumb	1st Finger	2nd Finger	3rd Finger	4th Finger
Right Hand					

	4th Finger	3rd Finger	2nd Finger	1st Finger	Thumb
Left Hand					

Birthmarks _____

_____

Scars _____

_____

Moles _____

_____

Special Physical Traits _____

_____

PRESCRIPTIONS SUMMARY FORM

Date	Name	Doctor	Reason	Rx Number	Details

PRESCRIPTIONS CURRENTLY TAKEN FORM

Reason	Date Begun	Date Ended	Doctor	Rx Name	Rx Dose/Frequency/ Directions

EMOTIONAL DUMP LIST

What's on My Mind?	What I Can Do about It!
_____	_____
_____	_____
_____	_____
_____	_____
_____	_____
_____	_____
_____	_____
_____	_____
_____	_____
_____	_____
_____	_____
_____	_____

SCHOOL CLOTHING INVENTORY

Name _____   Date _____

Type of Clothing	Number Needed	Number on Hand	Number to Purchase	Budget	Number Purchased	Actual Cost
Tops: short sleeve						
Tops: long sleeve						
Pants: short						
Pants: long						
Blouses: short sleeve						
Blouses: long sleeve						
Skirts						
Dresses						
Sweaters						
Socks						
Shoes						
Coats						
Boots						
Underwear						
Other						
Totals						

Notes

ACKNOWLEDGMENTS

A book is never the product of one individual's work. In the case of this book, it was the creation of a whole village including clients, audiences, friends, and professionals.

It included my editors at Cedar Fort, Allie Bowen and James Gallagher (who patiently listened when I made suggestions that sometimes made sense and other times were inconsistent with prevalent editing formats); my cover designer, Shawnda T. Craig (who listened when I wanted to add vibrant colors and a chrysanthemum to the cover); and my typesetter, Kaitlin Barwick (who was willing to simplify and unify the graphics, fonts, and the book layout to help more disorganized readers respond more easily to simplicity and repetition).

My acquisition editor, Briana Farr, kept me updated and enthusiastic about the project during the months of writing, editing, and proofing. Of course, the opportunity initially came because Esther Raty, Acquisition Specialist for Cedar Fort, approached me with the idea of publishing this book—and, although she has gone on to other professional pursuits, I am grateful for her early encouragement to make this book a reality.

And, my readers, clients, and listening audiences, I also include you in the village of people who have helped this book flower like a chrysanthemum. I have learned from you for many decades. Thanks for sharing, caring, and prodding me to great organizational capacities.

—— >> << ——

ABOUT THE AUTHOR

Marie has been sharing personal and home organization skills for thirty years. She teaches organization principles at professional and community gatherings, is a presenter at educational venues all over the United States, and has published several organization books. Marie has appeared as a featured guest on both TV and radio, has been a radio show host, and has helped men and women find greater organization skills in their personal and professional lives. She is currently a grief and loss psychotherapist in Mesa, Arizona, where she helps those who mourn find solace and comfort as they bring personal order into their lives again.

8 WEEKS TO AN ORGANIZED HOME

How to Organize Your Home and Keep It That Way

To enroll in the online course, scan to visit

learn.mothersniche.com/p/organize-home

MARIE'S OTHER ORGANIZATION E-BOOKS AND OTHER HELPFUL HOME-MANAGEMENT INFORMATION ARE ALSO AVAILABLE

To purchase these other materials, scan to visit

mothersniche.com